A PORTSMOUTH CANVAS

The Art of the City and the Sea 1770–1970

To Tessa
with Love from J.F.G.
Christmas 2014 .

A PORTSMOUTH CANVAS

The Art of the City and the Sea
1770–1970

NIGEL SURRY

'Whenever the weather permitted I would be off soon after breakfast, either to the Camber where I was certain of finding cargo boats, fishing vessels, sometimes a brig or schooner, or to some other part of the harbour, in search of vantage points from which to sketch warships. Sometimes I would cross the harbour by the Floating Bridge or Ferry Launch, and make a sketch from Clarence Square, Blockhouse Fort, or from the yacht building yards by Gosport Hard. For a change I would go by steamer to the Isle of Wight, Southampton or Buckler's Hard. Other congenial subjects were to be found on Langstone Harbour or at Portchester. Some of the paintings done that summer…are still in my possession. They carry my thoughts back to the days when they were painted and call up memories of that year.'

Peter Anson, *Harbour Head, Maritime Memories* (1945), p.165.

THE FORTUNE PRESS

Published by The Fortune Press

177 Melford Road, Sudbury,
Suffolk, CO10 1JU.

Text copyright Nigel Surry, 2008

ISBN 978-0-9559118-0-4

British Library Cataloguing in Publication Data
A catalogue record for this book is available from the British Library

Front Cover: Harry Coish, *Portsmouth Harbour*. Watercolour, 1881. Portsmouth City Museums.
Photographs from this collection reproduced with the kind permission of
Portsmouth Museums and Records Service.

Designed by Tina Ranft

Printed by Print Wright Ltd.,
Ipswich, IP1 5BN

September 2008

CONTENTS

ACKNOWLEDGEMENTS

I would like to thank the staff of the British Library Reference Division (formerly British Museum); the National Art Library, Victoria and Albert Museum; the National Register of Archives and Suffolk Libraries (Sudbury Branch).

Acknowledgement is made to the Association of Art Historians (Artists' Papers Register www.apr.ac.uk); the British Library, Department of Manuscripts for permission to quote from the *Journal* of the Reverend John Skinner, 1831; to the Imperial War Museum, Department of Art to quote from the J.D. Fergusson Archive, letter No.26 from J.D. Fergusson to Alfred Yockney 6th August 1918 and Eric Ravilious's letter to E.M. O'Dickey, 18th June 1940; the National Maritime Museum, Greenwich, Department of Manuscripts to quote from John Livesay's letter to an unknown correspondent, 17th January 1806; the Royal Academy of Arts, London to use extracts from James Northcote's letters to Samuel Northcote, 30th May & 30th June 1776 and William(?) Manley's letter to Ozias Humphrey, 17th July 1780; and likewise Essex Record Office, with regard to Caroline Wilkinson's *Journal* 1828; the Fergusson Gallery Archive for allowing me to quote from J.D. Fergusson's letter to Margaret Morris dated 1st August 1918; Hampshire Record Office regarding the Baigent family papers; Norfolk Record Office to quote from George Eaton's *Tour*, 1850; Michael Gunton, Acting Archivist, Portsmouth City Records Office for the generous use of their archives; the Royal Institution of Cornwall, to utilise John Swete's *Tour*, 1777; the University of Portsmouth kindly made the Art College Archives 1871–1998 available for my use. I would also like to thank the following who gave permission for publication of documents and other records in their possession: Tim Barringer, Roy Brinton, Maldwin Drummond, and the Right Reverend Raymond Jaconelli O.S.C.U., Nunraw Abbey, Haddington, Trustee of the Peter Anson Estate.

The following agreed to the use of extracts from published works: John Munday, *E.W. Cooke A Man of his Time* (Antique Collectors Club, Woodbridge, 1996), pp.275, 276, 280; Richard Shone editor, *The Burlington Magazine* Vol.136, No.1093, April 1994, pp.235, 236; Anne Ullman, *Ravilious at War* (The Fleece Press, Upper Denby, Huddersfield, 2002), pp.106, 109; Professor Richard Harding editor, *The Mariner's Mirror* Vol.48, No 4 Nov. 1962, pp.299; ibid 83 No.4 Nov. 1997, p.468; Louis Garneray (trans. Lawrence Wood), *The French Prisoner* (Merlin Press, 1957), pp.126–127; the Permissions Department, Oxford University Press, Anne Fremantle, *The Wynne Diaries,* Vol. III (1940), pp.61, 88, 89; Paget Toynbee and Leonard Whibley (eds.), *The Correspondence of Thomas Gray* Vol.1 (1971), p.48; Christina Colvin, *Maria Edgeworth: Letters from England 1813–1844* (1971), p.408; Ian Warrell, *Turner's Venice* Tate Britain Exhibition Catalogue, (Tate Publications, 2003), p.27; Yale University Press: A. Locknam, *The Etchings of James McNeill Whistler* (1984), p.239; Kathryn Cave, Kenneth Garlick and Angus Macintyre (eds.), *The Diary of Joseph Farington* (1978–1984), Vol.XIV, p.5080; Vol.XV, pp. 5258–5259; Nancy Marshall & Malcolm Warner, *James Tissot: Victorian Life/ Modern Love* (1999), p.82; Bernard Denvir, *The Late Victorians Art, Design and Society 1852–1910* (Pearson Education Ltd, 1980), pp.104, 242. I have been unable to trace the copyright holders of owners of works by Harry Coish (d.1925), George Horne (d. c.1940), Wilfrid Jefferies (d.1970),

Edward King (d.1951), Violet Pearse (d. c.1970); and the copyright of Sir Charles Oman's, *Memories Of Victorian Oxford And Of Some Early Years* (1941) and Peter Anson's *Harbour Head, Maritime Memories* (1945).

I would also like to thank those individuals and institutions who allowed illustrations to be used in this work or offered support in other respects, namely: the Ashmolean Museum, Oxford; the British Museum, Department of Prints and Drawings; the Fergusson Gallery, Perth; Gosport Museum; the Hunterian Museum and Art Gallery, University of Glasgow; the Imperial War Museum; the Moray Council Museum Service (Falconer Museum, Forres, Moray); the National Maritime Museum, Greenwich; the National Army Museum, Chelsea; the Norrish Central Library, Portsmouth; Pallant House Gallery, Chichester; the Paul Mellon Centre for Studies in British Art; Portsmouth City Museums and Records Service; the Portsmouth and Hampshire Art Society; the Portsmouth Naval Base Property Trust; Portsmouth Publishing and Printing Ltd; the Royal Institution of Cornwall, Truro; Tate Gallery Publishing Ltd, Tate Picture Library; Trafalgar Galleries, London; the University of Portsmouth; the University of Stirling; the Witt Library, Courtauld Institute, London; John Green, Maggie Neale, Garrick Palmer, Eric Rimmington and John Wyllie.

Particular thanks are reserved for those individuals whose help and encouragement has been of major importance in realising this enterprise, or who assisted with specific enquiries: Pauline Allwright; Lesley Burton; Emma Butterfield; Andrew Butterton; Jane Cameron; Ann Coates; Julie Cochrane; David Coke; Cheryl Crane; Deborah Croker; Hazel M. Farrell; David Francis; Bill Fulljames; Carlotta Gelmetti; Diana Grigg; Nigel Grundy; Margaret Hoad; Debbie Holland; Vicky Isley; Alasdair Joyce; Jennifer Kinnear; Cressida Kocinski; Margaret Lang; Emma Lauze; Lindsay Macfarlane; Julie McConnell; Sue Molineux; Anna Monro; Melissa Munro; Graham Nisbet; Anne Owen; Oonagh Palmer; Malcolm Pinhorn; Elizabeth Powis; Joanna Quill; Ray Riley; Pamela Robertson; Sarah and Mark Robinson; Claudia Schmid; Mike Shields; Catherine Smith; Kylie Storey; Barbara Thompson; Nigel Thorp; Anne Ullmann and Denise Williams. Kevin Purdy deserves particular mention for photographic work on my behalf since the late 1980s; John Webb for his time and trouble in commenting on the typescript; likewise, Pat Bray and Jane Lowe for reading the proofs; John Stedman and Katy Ball of Portsmouth City Museums, who, together with Sarah Quaill the former City Archivist, and the Record Office staff provided outstanding support at all times; likewise Alan King, Local Studies Librarian, and his colleagues at the Norrish Central Library. Any merit in the book's format is entirely due to the work of Tina Ranft the designer, Gill Robinson, and the staff at Print Wright.

On a more personal note, it would be churlish to forget the management of the former Dolphins Hotel and the Sallyport Inn for their hospitality. My thanks also to those friends who have patiently tolerated the frequent intrusion of Portsmouth's painters into general conversation, particularly Jenny White, John Lowe, Frank Ball and Mike Shaw. Polly Burns's encouragement and support have been invaluable throughout. As for the book, it is unreservedly dedicated to the memory of Geoffrey and Ada Jenkinson, who stayed me with flagons and comforted me with apples, for more years than I dare remember.

Nigel Surry, September 2008

(Note: Original spelling and punctuation are preserved in the quotations from primary sources. The references to plates in square brackets within the text represent the colour illustrations which are found in the separate colour section.)

INTRODUCTION

'The most sensible men I know (taken as a class) are painters; that is, they are the most lively observers in what passes in the world about them, and the closest observers of what passes in their own minds.' A.R. Walter and Arnold Clever (eds.), *The Collected Works of William Hazlitt* (London and New York 12v. 1903), VI, 'On The Pleasure Of Painting,' *Table Talk*, Essay I, p.10.

There were few years during Britain's heyday as a commercial and imperial power from the late eighteenth to early twentieth century, when a painting featuring Portsmouth was not on show at one of the principal London exhibitions, from William Bellars's *A View towards Cumberland Fort* (Free Society of Artists 1773), to Edwin Hayes's *Looking into Portsmouth* (Royal Academy 1904), and it is interesting to follow the changing fortunes of the city through the eyes of a host of painters, from Thomas Rowlandson to W.L. Wyllie and beyond.

The rise of the British School of Painters and the establishment of the Royal Academy, coincided with the expansion of Portsmouth under the Hanoverians, an importance that steadily increased in the century that followed. The town was well placed for travellers visiting the Isle of Wight and the New Forest, many stopping in the town, or passing through the immediate neighbourhood, their numbers swelling with the coming of the railways in the 1840s. Exponents of the picturesque, and later romantics found much to attract them in the views from Portsdown and the neighbouring Sussex Downs, while artistic interest in the Isle of Wight, at its highest between 1850 and 1870, was strengthened by the presence of Queen Victoria at Osborne, and fashionable interest in Cowes Week. The popularity of marine painting brought artists to

1. S. Manageot & Scotin, *View of the Town and Harbour of Portsmouth with His Majesty's Fleet under Sail, 1755* (Detail). Portsmouth City Museums.

the Solent in overwhelming numbers, and shipping in Portsmouth harbour, or at Spithead proved enduring subject material, increased by the town's association with frequent naval reviews from the 1770s onwards, as works by painters as distinctive as John Clevely, George Chambers and J.M. Whistler testify. But it was war or its imminent threat that was always a major reason for bringing artists to the town, in the Revolutionary and Napoleonic periods – Turner, Loutherbourg, Wilkie and Haydon to name but a few – establishing a pattern that was to last well into the twentieth century [Plate 1].

When the painter Carl Gustav Carus arrived in Portsmouth in 1844 with his master Frederick Augustus II King of Saxony, he dismissed Portsea Island, as 'a low marshy district.' Rather, it was what he saw from his room in the Commissioner's House in the Dockyard that took his eye:

> 'I soon found myself alone in the apartment…, and enjoyed from my window the view of this
> magnificent harbour, in which all the ships were covered with flags, and Admiral Nelson's ship, the
> *Victory*, was especially adorned with long rows of flags on all her masts. Before me stretched the vast
> dock – yards, magazines, and workshops, and in the distance the Isle of Wight, which shelters
> Spithead from the south winds, so celebrated as a safe anchorage for ships of war. Nothing but the
> necessity of a quick preparation for dinner could have forced me from the window.'

Many artists working in Portsmouth tended to follow Carus and look to the harbour and beyond. In the town itself, apart from the High Street with its shops, there was little to attract the visitor, unless he was content to observe the garrison at work and play:

> 'The omnibus rattles over iron drawbridges, and next, a dark subterranean arch admits you beneath
> the ramparts…Once within, fresh novelties strike the attention. A stately Highland soldier for
> instance is standing guard at the house of the Commander-in-Chief, and a bevy of the same fellows
> are standing at the barrack-gates, lounging after their morning sweat on the common. Then again, a
> little further on we see a group of middies and A.B. sailors assembled round the door of the
> George…But hark – there is military music! A regiment has passed from Penny-street towards its
> barracks…the brave 72nd are merrily trailing into barracks, to the sound of "should auld
> acquaintance" or "John Anderson my Joe…". '

Charpentier's *New Portsmouth & Southsea Guide* (1837), undoubtedly influenced by contemporary writers on the picturesque, is constantly urging the reader to look beyond the town itself, whether it be towards the upper harbour and Portchester from Flathouse, or out to sea from the earthworks (or glacis) opposite the newly built Bellevue Terrace, or from Fort Cumberland, as well as the more familiar Southsea Castle and the Platform. And it appears that painters responding to these ideas had little need to be persuaded, so little interest did they take in much of the developing town and its immediate neighbourhood. The countryside beyond was a different matter, revealing a continuity of interest and subject matter among artists of all kinds. A guidebook of the inter-war years extols Portchester and Netley for their ancient ruins and Rowlands Castle for its rural character, and recommends the view from Portsdown in terms that William Daniell and his contemporaries would have recognised [Plate 2], praising it as:

> 'a view of unceasing and ever charming character; a view that for all its evidence of the works of
> man, yet responds to every trick of the wind and light and every condition of the tide.'

Thus, when William Grant began painting rural scenes in the neighbourhood of Bedhampton, he was following a well established tradition. Paintings of houses and their gardens were fashionable in the 1920s and formed the basis of his livelihood, while the fact that Grant used mainly watercolour gave his work an intimacy and informality that struck a chord with the wider public. He returned to paint Langstone Mill, on Portsea Island, a popular beauty spot, on several occasions – one of the earliest surviving versions is dated 1910 when he was only 17 years old, although much of his later work derived from his affection for the country between Warblington and Chichester [Plate 3].

In the late 19th and early 20th centuries the public became far more receptive to pictures of commercial and industrial activities and wider aspects of everyday life. There was a focus on the Camber Dock, with its cargo and fishing boats, and more on the Dockyard in works by local painters including W.E. Atkins, Harry Coish, and W.A. Jefferies. The rise of the Empire greatly added to Portsmouth's importance, and by late Victorian times Southsea possessed most if not all the trappings of a seaside resort, though few painters were attracted to this aspect of the town's life, the majority preferring traditional marine subjects, perhaps scarcely surprising given the importance of the Royal Navy. The two World Wars had a far greater effect on artists as distinctive as W.L. Wyllie, Edward King and Eric Ravilious in their choice of subject matter, while Portsmouth's late 20th century role as a university town, and tourist centre have in turn created new possibilities.

Portsmouth maintains a tradition of marine painting going back to the presence of the Naval Academy. Local talent for much of the last two hundred years has been largely overshadowed by that of outsiders, further compounded by the departure to London of the more able or ambitious artists, for reasons that will become clear. Yet it is surely worthwhile to ask why painters came to Portsmouth and in some cases spent much of their working lives here. What opportunities did the place and its neighbourhood hold for them? What influence (if any) did it have on their work? An attempt has been made to answer these questions, as far as possible from contemporary letters, diaries, memoirs, newspapers and other records – voices from the past, above all, where possible, those of the artists themselves, and of course their work. It is hoped that this approach will appeal as much to art historians as to those with a wider interest in Portsmouth and its history.

CHAPTER 1

PORTSMOUTH REVEALED: TOWN, DOCKYARD AND PEOPLE

'It is now the only regular fortification in the Kingdom, and may with propriety be called the *Key of England.*' In these words, Lake Taswell author of *The Portsmouth Guide* (1775), sums up the town's importance and one of its chief attractions, adding a visit to the Dockyard in the nearby suburb of Portsea, a tour of one of the King's ships, and the pleasure of watching reviews of the fleet, and from time to time, the arrival and departure of naval expeditions [Plate 4]. The Portsmouth portrayed in the guidebook – the earliest of its kind – was a bustling place with well paved streets, 'three elegant inns, the George, Fountain and King's Arms, as well as 'a very good Coffee-house on the Grand Parade, called the Crown.' There was a theatre at the upper end of the High Street used for assemblies in the winter months, and in nearby Portsea, concert rooms. Since 1754 a bathing house had been open to subscribers. This was situated on the Point and boasted 'four fine baths of different depths of water' and 'two good dressing rooms.'

Few visitors needed much urging to look at the view from the Saluting Platform and the ramparts, which offered 'one of the most striking variegable scenes imaginable'. After settling his accommodation, the American Louis Simond and his friends 'took a walk along the walls, which are the resort

2. Dominic Serres, *George III Reviewing the Fleet, Spithead*, 1786. Portsmouth City Museums.

3. James Calcott, *Market House and Guildhall*, n.d. Portsmouth City Museums.

of the beau monde, and from whence there is a fine sea view, Spithead and all the ships at anchor'
[Plate 5]. A look inside the parish church of St Thomas's in the High Street was also part of the
established itinerary. By the end of the eighteenth century, the appearance of the street itself was rapidly
changing, many of the old half-timbered buildings 'having within the last few years either [been] rebuilt
or new-fronted'; although it was not until 1837 that the old Town Hall and market house in the centre
of the road was demolished and rebuilt on the south side next to the Dolphin. By then, thanks to these
changes there was some justification in the High Street being described as 'very handsome, adorned with
many excellent shops', and its growing popularity with painters and engravers.

From the 1770s visitors came in growing numbers, including painters, generally as part of a tour
of the Solent area in search of picturesque scenery. Many such expeditions took in Southampton, the
New Forest and the Isle of Wight, concluding with a brief stay in Portsmouth before the homeward
journey, or the route was reversed. In the next hundred years the town continued to expand beyond
its ancient fortifications leading to further development in Portsea with the continuing expansion of
the Dockyard, and the emergence of new suburbs, Landport to the north and Southsea to the east,

all within the geographical area of Portsea Island, much of which was low lying, given over to agriculture or marshland.

The review of the fleet at Spithead by George III that began on 22nd June 1773 was an elaborately staged affair, and recounted in some detail in Taswell's book:

> 'His Majesty went from the dockyard at half an hour after five this morning to view the new works and fortifications…beginning from the farthest part of the common round to the saluting platform. At seven [he] returned to the dock, embarked immediately on board the Augusta yacht, and sailed out of the harbour, the fortifications saluting as he passed…proceed [ing] as far as Sandown Bay, where the Standard was saluted by the Castle…After the King had sailed along the line of ships remaining at Spithead, he stood towards the harbour, and came to anchor about half a mile within Southsea-Castle, where His Majesty was attended by the admiral, rear-admiral and all the captains and lieutenants of the fleet at Spithead, who had severally the honour of kissing [his] hand. While the yacht was at anchor, the ramparts of the town, being lined with land-forces and marines, fired a 'Feu de Joy' at ten o'clock, by a triple discharge of cannon and musquetry all round the works; immediately after which the yacht was weighed, proceeded into the harbour and landed His Majesty at the dock at half an hour after ten o'clock.'

It was the first of several to be commemorated by the King's Marine Painter Dominic Serres and exhibited at the recently founded Royal Academy in London. The original series of four is still part of the Royal collection, but various copies were made. A drawing of the yacht *Augusta* made by the young Thomas Luny may have been used in his master Francis Holman's interpretation of the same event, shown at the Academy in 1774. Yet another version by John Clevely senior was also on view, and a painting of the Dockyard by Richard Paton and John Hamilton Mortimer, also in the Queen's collection and dating from c.1775, are further reminders of Portsmouth's importance. Many years earlier Daniel Defoe described the 'Docks and Yards' as:

> 'like a Town by themselves, and are a kind of Marine Corporation, or a Government of their own kind within themselves; there being particular large rows of dwellings, built at the publick Charge, within the New Works, for all the principal Officers of the Place; especially the Commissioner, the Agent of Victualling, and such as these; the Tradesmen likewise have houses here, and many of the Labourers are allow'd to live in the bounds as they can get Lodging.'

The launching of ships, and the ceremonial associated with them were a feature of the town's daily life, particularly during wartime, combining elements of patriotism and civic pride, frequently the subject of engravings, as in Joshua Cristall's *Launch of the 'Prince of Wales'* (1794) which showed:

> 'The Royal Family, with their suites and attendants…placed under a rich canopy in an admirable situation to observe the whole process. The different officers and servants of the dockyard attended in their respective departments, and the whole harbour was covered with boats and vessels with bands of music. She was christened by Prince Adolphus, who threw a bottle of claret on her side as she majestically approached the liquid surface of the deep, amidst the plaudits of tens of thousands of admiring spectators.'

Paintings of the town, shipping in the harbour and neighbouring landscapes were becoming more popular, although little is known about the activities of local painters before the 1770s, and no recognisable group of indigenous artists emerges until the 1820s.

4. Joshua Cristall, *The Launch of the 'Prince of Wales' before their Majesties at Portsmouth,* 1794. Portsmouth City Museums.

As well as exploring nearby Portchester with its ruined castle, Taswell's guide assumes tourists will be eager to visit neighbouring country houses at Purbrook, Southwick and Stansted, to inspect their grounds and art collections, and beyond that, Gosport with its newly opened Haslar Hospital, Fareham, and possibly explore the Isle of Wight. It praised the view from Portsdown Hill, but in this respect it lagged well behind certain poets and painters. As early as c.1730, Robert Griffier painted a *View of Portsmouth* close to where the old London Road crosses the hill near the George Inn, a favourite spot with artists well into the nineteenth century and beyond, while Griffier's contemporary, Thomas Gray, described what he saw possibly from the same place:

> '...to the South, Portsmouth, Gosport &c, just at your feet in appearance, the Fleet, the sea winding
> & breaking in bays into the land, the deep shade of tall Oaks in the enclosure, in wch you plainly
> distinguish the fields, hedgerows & woods next the shore, and a backdrop of hills behind them.
> I have not seen a more magnificent or more varied prospect.'

When he was a young unknown artist, Joshua Reynolds came to Portsmouth in 1744 at the height of the War of the Austrian Succession (1739–1748), 'to paint naval officers at a guinea apiece', for whatever a painter's aspirations, portrait painting was the most reliable way of making money. The town was rising in prosperity and continued to profit greatly from the European and Colonial wars of the period, and even George III's disastrous attempt to subdue the rebellious American settlers brought prosperity in its wake, if this contemporary comment is to be believed:

> 'Few places are at present [1781] more flourishing than this: the great sums of prize money spent by
> the sailors, added to the wages constantly laid out by the number of hands employed in the
> Dockyard cause a greater circulation of cash than is to be found in most parts of the Kingdom.'

5. Long Row, The Parade, Portsmouth Dockyard. Portsmouth Naval Base Property Trust.

Reynolds's example was followed some years later in May 1776 by one of his former assistants, James Northcote, in his own words at the invitation of 'my friend Mr Hunt, at that time Master Builder in the Dock Yard there and afterwards Surveyor of the Navy'. Hunt, as a senior official was well placed to help Northcote, who also benefited from being invited to stay at Hunt's home, one of a terrace, Long Row, built for dockyard officers between 1716 and 1719 that survives to this day. Northcote began by painting members of his host's family, his confidence gradually increasing with their encouragement, as he explained to his brother Samuel in Plymouth:

> 'I have finish'd Mr Hunt, and it is thought very like and am now doing his youngest Child sleeping and I like it myself the best of any I have done and he is mightily pleased with it.'

This was just as well, since in these early weeks, few if any appeared to take advantage of Northcote's presence leading him to conclude, 'the people here have if possible less relish for pictures than at Plymouth.' But by the end of June he was pleased to confide in his brother, that he 'made use of all the day light to paint as I am kept very busy.' Among his sitters were naval and military officers and their families, clergy, government officials and contractors – a good cross section of that middling element in society that played such a large part in the cultural life of many Georgian towns. (See Appendix 1, below). Northcote became wholly captivated by the ladies of one particular family, the Prossers, boasting:

'I have just done a picture of the two Mis Prossers who are the most beautiful girls in all Portsmh and are the most sensible and best bredd women I now they entertain me While I paint by playing on the hapsicord and singing most delightfully.'

He describes going with them to the theatre and on another occasion joining them for 'junket and strawberries', and was even invited to stay with the family at their cottage on the Isle of Wight. Fortunately the painter also found time, perhaps taking advice from Lake Taswell, to walk the town ramparts, sail up the harbour to explore the ruins of Portchester Castle, and closer at hand inspect the Gunwharf, look over ships and other sights in the Dockyard including the Observatory attached to the Naval Academy, where he witnessed an eclipse of the moon. Northcote also visited the Concert Rooms in St George's Square, where he painted a portrait of the proprietor Moses Hawker, the town organist.

On 30th May, with the ever obliging Hunt he was driven 'six miles in the country in a chaise' to Purbrook Park to meet its owner Peter Taylor Esq., one of the town's two M.Ps, and view his host's art collection. The meeting was not a success, and the tone of Northcote's account suggests he may have been disappointed in the hope for a commission:

'Mr Taylor…is very rich and has built a fine house but is a very Ignorant man…he show'd us his pictures which he thinks a fine collection but are really not worth six pence one in particular a Copy from the Cornaro family Of Titian which he thinks a true one which if so would be worth 12 Thousand pounds but very bad. Another picture in which were a vast number of men at work with carts waggons and horses some driving of piles and seem'd to be building a pier. He told us it was the entry of Harry the Eighth in to Callis.'

Northcote's brief excursion to the Isle of Wight in August had more fortunate results. He had been invited by the Reverend Leonard Troughear Holmes, painting portraits of his hosts, who very kindly took him over the Island, where among the various collections on show, Northcote singled out that of Sir Richard Worsley's at Appledurcombe, later famous for its range of old masters and sculptures from the ancient world. When he went back to Plymouth that September Northcote took with him about £150, and following further success at home set out for Italy, for long the object of every ambitious painter, where he remained for three years, returning in 1780.

Not all artists or their friends were as relatively uncritical of the town as Northcote. There were frequent grumbles at the expense of food and lodgings and the often squalid state of the streets. One

6. James Northcote, *Self Portrait*, 1784. National Portrait Gallery, London.

ABOVE: 7. Thomas Malton, *South West View of Purbrook in Hampshire,* c.1770. Ashmolean Museum, University of Oxford.
BELOW: 8. *Catalogue of the Worsley Collection* (Title Page), 1804. Private Collection.

traveller grumbled that only Bath and Canterbury were more expensive than Portsmouth, and another who stayed at the King's Arms, complained that during his short stay, he had had wretched accommodation and been grossly over-charged. The painter Thomas Jones, whilst staying at the King's Arms in 1773, left his sketchbook on the dining room table, to return only to find that several drawings had been stolen. But among the most scathing criticisms were those made by William (?) Manley, stranded at Portsmouth while awaiting passage with a convoy to India in July 1780, in this letter to his friend the artist Ozias Humphry:

> 'You cannot imagine how disagreeable it is to live in Portsmouth which of all others is the most odious & the most detestable place I ever put my head into. St Giles's itself never exhibited such scenes of vice and abandoned wickedness as Portsmouth does daily. The common Prostitutes exceed every idea of prostitution that I ever heard of or cod have conceived, & the Inhabitants are a very lazy, impudent, imposing set of people.'

CATALOGUE RAISONNÉ

OF THE PRINCIPAL

PAINTINGS, SCULPTURES, DRAWINGS,
&c. &c.

AT APPULDURCOMBE HOUSE,

THE SEAT OF THE

RT. HON. SIR RICHARD WORSLEY, BART.

TAKEN JUNE 1, 1804.

" The practice of Architecture is directed by a few general, and even mechanical rules. But Sculpture, *and above all,* Painting, propose to themselves the imitation not only of the forms of nature, but of the characters and passions of the human soul. In those sublime arts, the dexterity of the hand is of little avail, unless it is animated by fancy, and guided by the most correct taste and observation." GIBBON.

LONDON:

PRINTED BY WILLIAM BULMER AND CO.
CLEVELAND-ROW, ST. JAMES'S.
1804.

9. George Brannon,
*Appledurcombe
House*, 1828.
Private Collection.

The seamier side of life and much more were captured by Thomas Rowlandson, whose drawings bring to life a town 'where everything breathes and smells of soldiers, sailors and docksmen' quite unlike any painter before or since. The text of his *Tour* (1784) has unfortunately disappeared, but the surviving pen and ink drawings suggest that Rowlandson and his friend Henry Wigstead spent two days at Portsmouth at the end of a jaunt covering Salisbury, Lyndhurst, Lymington and Cowes, providing a vivid chronicle of their activities, including boarding HMS *Hector,* and the scene below decks showing sailors lounging about, playing cards or carousing with their womenfolk; the two

10. Thomas
Rowlandson,
*Going on board the
'Hector' of 74 Guns,
lying in Portsmouth
Harbour,* 1782.
© National Maritime
Museum, Greenwich,
London.

11. Thomas Rowlandson, *Jack Ratlin's Tavern, Portsmouth,* 1784/1805. Portsmouth City Museums.

friends relaxing over supper at their inn; the site of the *Royal George*, masts or spars protruding above the water, and a rather empty and subdued drawing of the Point that has little in common with the better known *Portsmouth Point* (c.1800), or its reputed companion piece, *Portsmouth Harbour.* Perhaps the boisterous *Jack Ratlin's Tavern* (1784/1805) was worked up from a preliminary sketch made at this time although it is certain that Rowlandson came to Portsmouth on more than one occasion.

He is known to have travelled down from London following Lord Howe's victory over the French, the Glorious First of June, 1794 to witness Howe's arrival with his captured enemy prizes, recording this event from the Saluting Platform as the ships entered the harbour, brilliantly evoking the mood of the occasion as a motley crowd of veterans, ladies of fashion, unruly children and officers with telescopes, jostle one another to get the best view. Nothing could be in sharper contrast than an incident that took place shortly afterwards, recalled by Henry Angelo who was with the painter when wounded French prisoners were landed at Gosport and loaded into carts:

> 'The sudden jolting made their groans appalling…The sight was dreadful to behold; numbers were boys, mutilated, some not more than twelve years old, who had lost both legs. In the evening we went to Forton Prison. Those who were not in the last engagement, were in high spirits, in their shops, selling all sorts of toys and devices, made from shin-bones &c. In one of the sick wards we saw one of the prisoners, who, an officer told us, had been a tall, handsome man, previous to the battle; but, having received a shot that had lacerated his side, a mortification had taken place. He was then making his will; his comrades were standing by, consoling him, some grasping his hand, shedding tears.'

This scene proved too much for Angelo and he left… 'but I could not persuade Rowlandson to follow me, his inclination to make a sketch of the dying moment getting the better of his feelings.' Rowlandson eventually joined his friend, having:

12. Thomas Rowlandson, *Lord Howe's Victory, or French Prizes Brought into Portsmouth Harbour*, 1794. V&A Images/ Victoria And Albert Museum, London.

'produced a rough sketch of what he had seen:- a ghastly figure, sitting up in bed, a priest holding a crucifix before him, with a group standing behind. The interior exhibited the contrivance of the French to make their prison habitable. When finished, it was added to my collection, a momento of the shocking sight I beheld at Forton Prison.'

The Dying Sailor, produced a few years earlier 1787/90, is a far less realistic representation of such an incident, although in an uncanny way it anticipates this event. Angelo returned to London the next day, leaving his friend who went to Southampton to see the departure of an expeditionary force to aid the French royalists of La Vendée.

A third contemporary, the Reverend John Swete, also included Portsmouth in his tour during the summer of 1777. He marvelled at the wonders of the Dockyard, particularly the Smithy where he saw an anchor being made, and true Augustan that he was, would certainly have agreed with the Gosport historian Comyns, that the Dockyard 'stands unrivalled, both in the annals of Roman Grandeur, and on a comparative view of modern improvements'. Swete arrived with his friends by boat from Southampton in August and despite seasickness, a source of great amusement to them, set out the same evening to walk the ramparts. It was the time of the annual Free Mart Fair and the town was looking at its best. He rejoiced at the sight of:

'the fair inhabitants of the place deckt out in their Sunday-going Cloaths, and crowding through the Streets. It was the last Day of a fair and all was Mirth and Revelry. The Jovial Tar had put on his best blue Jacket and his white Cotton Stockings; and seem'd to vie with the spruce Mechanic for the

13. William Westall, *Netley Abbey*, n.d. Portsmouth City Museums.

Affections of the Fille de chambre whether it "Blew high or Blew low" he regarded not; but in his present Enjoyments neither anticipated future Evils, or recall'd those that were past.'

Swete had been greatly impressed by Haslar Hospital, reputedly the largest brick building in Europe, which he sketched in watercolour 'from the Great Cabbin of the *Royal George*', and described and drew Southsea Castle, but his main interest lay in landscape, preferably if it included 'gothic' antiquities such as Netley Abbey, which he enthused over at some length in his journal [Plate 6]. Portsmouth could not compete in these respects, but even so he included these remarks to accompany his views of the Castle and nearby Common:

> 'The Country around Portsmouth is by no means unpleasant – rather indeed too Open to afford any striking natural Prospects. Some of the scenes however not altogether destitute of Picturesque Beauty. The Sketch on the opposite Page was taken on my return from Southsea Castle; it hath a distant view on the left of a shaded walk of Trees on the Fortifications of the Town, with an adjacent Windmill, and terminated by very remote Hills rising one above the Other.'

Late Georgian Portsmouth clearly provoked very different reactions from all three men: the timid but determined Northcote, as generally cautious in his behaviour as he was conventional in these early portraits; the exuberant, worldly Rowlandson; and the kindly Swete, absorbed in his search for the picturesque and interest in antiquities, but not wholly at the expense of the world around him.

CHAPTER 2

PORTSMOUTH REVEALED: CONSTRAINTS AND DIVERSIONS

The responses of Northcote, Rowlandson and Swete to Portsmouth tell us much, but inevitably not the whole story, either in words or pictures. There were things the three men did not see, or considered worth recording, or that bypassed them altogether. Perhaps Rowlandson was closest to the harsher aspects of life, certainly the lot of the French prisoners held not only at Forton but also at Portchester Castle and in various hulks at the upper end of the harbour, where they proved a source of curiosity to visitors of all kinds. Betsy Fremantle, wife of Captain Fremantle, was with her husband and a party of fellow naval officers at Portchester in August 1801, writing in her diary:

> 'Went to Portchester Castle in the barge…saw the French prisoners & bought several of their ingenious works, went round to Fareham in the barge where we dined…We amused ourselves very well, & found it very pleasant coming back to Portsmouth, but once stuck in the mud & the tide then falling there fast we were on the point of remaining there all night, had it not been for Capt. Foley's exertions, who in the dread of remaining in that disagreeable situation all night took possession of one of the oars, and we got off.'

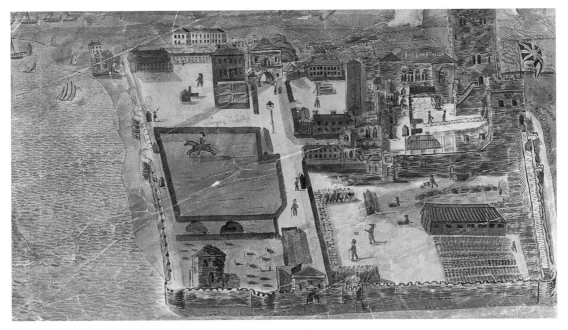

14. Anon, *A Bird's Eye View of Portchester Castle Nov. 1817*. Portsmouth City Museums.

Two years later, 25th August 1803, the expedition was repeated with only one minor incident:

> '…We went in a wherry and called on board the *Sultana* Hulk where the French prisoners are kept, 360 of them. I only saw some on deck who looked perfectly happy, noisy and talkative as usual. We carried a very good cold dinner with us to Porchester, and Mrs Kidson allowed us to make use of one of her rooms, a dismal one like every thing else belonging to these old walls, where however we ate with very good appetite and after seeing a Buffalo Bull by the Regiment of Dragoons just returned to this country, we got into our little hired boat and came to Portsea. Walking home poor Justine received such a hard pinch from a sailor that passed us, that she was quite frightened.'

It was the misfortune of a French painter, Louis Garneray, to be held prisoner on board the hulks between 1806 and 1814 [Plate 7]. The actual harshness of the living conditions led Garneray, who came from an artistic background to begin painting and earn himself some money, as prisoners had some latitude in this respect. At first he turned to portraiture, painting the guards, for an average price of 6d. to a 1s., but he is now remembered as a marine artist. A watercolour of c.1810 *Prison Hulks in Portsmouth Harbour* combines the two worlds that he knew for so long, that of the prison epitomised by the grim line of hulks anchored one behind the other in a straight line in contrast to the yachts of sightseers zig zagging as they wished amongst them. Yet as Garneray's account of his first meeting with a local dealer makes clear, even this existence was not without its lighter moments:

> 'One day I was visited by a little round man, who came uninvited into my humble studio and began to look at my pictures in the most brazen manner, without a word to me!
> "These seascapes," he said at last, are not bad at all for a Frenchman. If you are inclined to be reasonable perhaps we can come to some sort of agreement. I am a dealer in Portsea."
> As I was very short of money at that time I thought I saw heaven opening before me and I hastened to assure him that in matters of business I was not at all a difficult sort of person…
> After a short discussion it was agreed that he would take all my pictures, on condition that they were of a certain size and finish, at one pound or twenty-five francs apiece. I was overjoyed at his offer, which I had not in the least expected. I received six pounds that very day for the pictures he found in my studio and took away with him.'

The painter David Wilkie came to Portsmouth in September 1808 to visit his brother, an army officer, stationed there. It was not a happy experience for either, so it seems, if we are to believe Wilkie's biographer, David Cunningham:

> 'He dined with his brother and the officers in the mess and disliked their conversation which was all of a martial character: nor did he think it improved by the admission of some naval officers who gave it a maritime turn…On his way by Gosport to London he visited the place where the works of the French prisoners were exposed for sale: he was astonished with the ingenuity of that people, he said, but disgusted with the want of delicacy and modesty in some of their productions. He made another attempt to enjoy an evening with the military comrades of his brother at Portsmouth; but found them too convivial and boisterous, and took the road to London…'

Wilkie was something of a prig, yet pictures such as *The Blind Fiddler*, with their clear debt to Dutch seventeenth century genre painting, clearly touched the public imagination. The novelist Maria Edgeworth, exploring her son's ship at Portsmouth in 1822 was moved to write, 'Between decks in the *Phaeton* we saw the men at dinner with their wives – an admirable scene for Wilkie.' A scene, alas, that he was destined never to paint.

The following year Wilkie was invited to Plymouth by his friend and fellow artist, Benjamin Robert Haydon, the pair setting out from Portsmouth in June, when the Walcheron expedition was in the final stages of preparation [Plate 8]. They were reluctant eyewitnesses to the aftermath of a serious explosion on the beach, that had been caused:

> 'by a woman striking her pipe against some of the soldiers' baggage, among which some powder had been carelessly spilt; the loose powder caught, ran along the beach and around the baggage, blew up the broken barrel, which in its turn blew up all the barrels…(about a dozen), as well as the sergeant and his guard placed there to prevent any accident.'

By the afternoon the pair had sufficiently recovered from the shock to go and see the fleet at Spithead, prompting Haydon to reflect:

> 'What a sublime and terrible simplicity there is in our navy! Nothing is admitted but what is absolutely useful. The cannon, the decks, the sailors, all wore the appearance of stern vigour, as if constituted only to resist the elements. No beautiful forms in the gun-carriages, no taste or elegance in the cannon; the ports square and hard; the guns iron; the sailors muscular. Everything inspired one with awe'.

How different a standpoint this is, from a later generation affected by the romance of sail. True, he was overcome by the grandeur presented by the fleet, 350 men of war and transports, but individually Haydon found them useful rather than beautiful.

Whatever mishaps befell Haydon and Wilkie, at least they travelled in comfort, unlike John Britton, who arrived in the town in the summer of 1798 when it was full of troops and all the inns and public houses were full [Plate 9]. Thus, 'compelled to practice economy,' he was forced to find a lodging house for the night:

> '…at length I went to a shop in a back street, where "lodgings for travellers" was placarded. Here I was shown a room where six or eight beds were placed side by side, some of which were occupied by one or two persons. Remembering the old proverb of "honour among thieves", I chose one of these humble couches rather than go further and perhaps fare worse. In my travelling attire and unwashed, I laid myself on a sort of straw pallet, beneath a horse-cloth for a counterpane, and, being over-fatigued with a long day's walk, quickly became insensible of danger and of fellow-lodgers. But I was shortly roused from slumber by a Babylonish confusion of tongues and sounds; for the room was filled with human beings: old and young, male and female, drunk and sober, rough and rude, gentle and simple. Having chosen an extreme corner of the room, and a narrow bed to carry one person, I was not intruded on by later visitants, who unceremoniously laid themselves down wherever they could see a small space unoccupied. Quarrelling, swearing, crying, intreating, mixed with a few hard blows, were heard and felt, whilst hearty prayers and curses came from other mouths. My next neighbours were an old woman, and a younger one with an infant, whose lamentations and grief were poignant and heart-felt. The first had lost a son, the second a husband, and the third a father, facts which were proclaimed by the ejaculations of the speakers, and by the cries of the child. However I might lament and pity the sufferers, and these minor horrors and calamities of war, I could not but feel disgusted at the brutal language of some of my recumbent neighbours, who cursed and anathematised the poor sufferers for disturbing their repose. This night's lodging cost me sixpence, from having the sole occupancy of one bed, whilst those who joined in partnership of two or three were accommodated on lower terms.'

Britton was travelling on foot to Chepstow and London and back, collecting materials for the early volumes of *The Beauties of England and Wales* (1801–1816). The Hampshire volume published in 1805 included two of his own drawings, *Cuffnells* and *Netley Castle and Abbey*, and, as editor, he later commissioned works from artists as varied as Neale, Turner and Dayes. Like Garneray, early setbacks were a prelude to a successful career.

But for how many of the convicts, who were such a feature of Portsmouth at this time was this the case? Betsy Fremantle saw them working at Fort Cumberland, after visiting the camp at Southsea Castle on 2nd September 1803, and was obviously affected by the experience:

> '..it is a melancholy sight to see so many wretches at work with heavy chains to their feet. And I was much shocked to discover among them numbers of quite young Lads fourteen or fifteen years of age.'

Few travellers paid them any attention, but in 1831 the antiquarian Elisha Davy noted that 700 of them were working in the Dockyard, in brownish coloured uniforms, lightly supervised, shackled on one leg only, mostly sweeping up and on general cleaning duties, working in gangs.

Usually it was only attempted escapes and the accompanying violence that drew them to the notice of the public, most dramatically in 1810 when between 200 and 300 of them unsuccessfully attempted to break out from Fort Cumberland. Convicts continued to be used as a labour force in the town well into the nineteenth century. For the soldiers called in to quell these disturbances life was just as brutal in many respects. The same Portsdown Hill which gave such pleasure to artists and travellers alike was the site of a firing squad in 1802, when up to 15,000 troops under the command of General Whitelocke were assembled from the Isle of Wight, Chichester and elsewhere to witness the public execution of deserters from the garrison. Flogging was not abolished until the army reforms of the late 1860s, while deserters continued to be branded with a 'D' until 1879.

However, the harshness of everyday life for many, particularly during the war years, was eased, to a certain extent, by public spectacles and entertainments (including the Free Mart Fair), featuring the work of artists, notably transparencies and panoramas. Transparencies had long been a feature in pleasure gardens such as Vauxhall, and as part of theatrical productions, and more widely in illuminated tableaux, often accompanied by bonfires and fireworks in celebration of national events. George III's recovery from madness in 1789 led to widespread public rejoicing, in which Portsmouth took part as a matter of course:

> 'The whole Common displayed a blaze of illuminations. The Commissioner's house, and all the officers of the Dock-yard, Gunwharf Armoury, Victualling Office, Royal Hospital &c &c., were richly lighted up. Nor can we leave unnoticed a beautiful transparent painting, set off in an Elegant stile, at Mr Edward Brine's in Queen Street, representing the King and Queen in the centre of a large oval held up by Fame, whose Trumpet proclaimed, '*God preserve the Royal Pair*'.'

The celebrations that followed Trafalgar gave Richard Livesay, a local artist, an opportunity to design several in the aftermath of the battle, the earliest of which is described in considerable detail in the *Hampshire Telegraph*:

> 'We particularly noticed Admiral Montagu's in which was represented a naval crown (designed and neatly painted by Mr Livesay) encircled with branches of laurel, and in the centre the inscription, 'Victory', a pillar on the top of which stood a vase, adorned with laurel branches, with the

15. Sir Robert Ker Porter, *The Storming of Seringapatam, 1799*. Courtesy of the Director, National Army Museum, London.

following inscription: *'Nelson Immortal.'* At the base was the figure of Britannia, lamenting *the decease* of her hero – the French and Spanish colours lying at her feet. In the background a stern view of the Victory: a distant fleet and the departing sun. The urn on this occasion was most happily introduced, to show that in the midst of rejoicing, the nation's loss was not forgotten.'

A month later a concert was held at Portsmouth Theatre in aid of the widows and children bereaved at Trafalgar for which Livesay agreed 'to produce some characteristic paintings and transparencies' and at a further concert in March 1806, to include music by Handel:

'A Grand Transparency will be exhibited, designed, appointed and presented by Mr Livesay, on which some of the leading features of the *Glorious Battle Off Trafalgar* will be portrayed, with the Apotheosis of Lord Nelson'.

An exhibition of Livesay's work was held at the Concert Rooms in St George's Square to raise money for Lloyd's Patriotic Fund in the same month, and to 'The Apotheosis of Lord Nelson', were added, 'the Action Off Trafalgar and the battle of the Nile' to which a musical accompaniment was provided by the band of the North Hants Militia.

In 1814, as part of the entertainment given to the Prince Regent and the visiting Allied Sovereigns, a huge transparency, 'the whole containing an area of 230 superficial feet', was displayed at the Crown Inn, High Street, 'the work of Mr Bird, decorative painter at the Portsmouth Theatre', showing:

'…the Royal Arms, supported by those of Russia and Prussia…with the names Alexander, Platoff, Frederick William, Blucher…emanating from a radiant glory, dispersing with opaque clouds in every direction, the whole resting upon a pedestal, at the top of which was a Dove irridated by glory, emerging from the clouds, and bearing the olive branch…On the lower base a palm branch, and on the sinister a laurel encompassing the name Wellington…'

Among the most impressive spectacles to appear in the town was surely Robert Ker Porter's, 'The Panorama of the great Historical Picture descriptive of the storming of Seringapatam' painted in 1800, and exhibited at the Lyceum Theatre in London, and at Portsmouth in March 1807, at the Tennis Court, 'adjoining the White Swan, Halfway houses.' Admission cost a shilling, a commentary was provided as well as a booklet for one shilling and sixpence. This panorama was an enormous work, containing 'two thousand five hundred and fifty square feet of canvas (with) upwards of seven hundred figures as large as life, with portraits of British officers', completed so it was claimed in six weeks. It was later destroyed by fire, but a series of engravings by John (?) Thompson give some idea of its complexity. This was the first of several on similar themes, and appropriate in another sense, for the artist had already presented his painting *Christ stilling a storm on the Sea of Galilee* (1796), to the Roman Catholic Chapel in Prince George Street. Naval and military subjects continued to appeal to the public throughout the war period and beyond. Marshall's panorama of 'the Battles of Ligny, Les Quatres Bras and Waterloo' was followed a few years later in 1824 by 'the Bombardment of Algiers by Lord Exmouth', while in contrast 'the north Pole (Captain Parry's last voyage)' also proved popular with local people.

CHAPTER 3

THE NAVAL ACADEMY
AND ITS DRAWING MASTERS

16. John Lee, *Royal Naval College, Portsmouth*, 1806. Portsmouth City Museums.

By the early eighteenth century, drawing was already a professional requirement for naval and military officers, so it is not surprising that several naval officers were among the few resident painters to be found in Portsmouth in the late eighteenth century, apart from several profilists, including John Lea 'late of the Parade', active in the town for most of the war period. The best known from a naval background are Captain William Elliott, among whose surviving works are two oil paintings of the harbour c.1790, and Captain Robert Elliott, a relation, who painted a watercolour of *Crown Street* (1810). The Royal Naval Academy at Portsmouth Dockyard established in 1729 had a resident drawing master on the staff, and a drawing of the Academy c.1806 is ascribed to John Lee, a pupil working there from 1800–1802. Another student, William Carthew's surviving 'Plan of Mathematical Learning' (1774) introduces each section, on topics as varied as Astronomy, Geography and Fortifica-

17. William Carthew, *An Imaginary (?) Landscape, from 'A Plan of Mathematical Learning Taught in the Royal Academy Portsmouth Performed by William Carthew A Student there 1774'* (Detail). Portsmouth City Records Office.

tion, with a series of over 20 drawings mainly in pen, ink and wash, generally featuring a lake, with a backdrop of hills, and an island crowned by a church or small settlement with a farm or outbuildings, sometimes fortified. Are they the product of imagination? Or perhaps reminders of a holiday spent around the Swiss or Italian Lakes? Or an integral part of the 'Plan'? The drawing master at this time was the little known J(ohn)? Jeffrey. Several of his successors had wider talents that brought them into the public eye, particularly Richard Livesay, 'portrait and marine painter' and John Christian Schetky 'marine painter in ordinary' to George IV, William IV and Queen Victoria.

When Livesay was appointed in 1796 he was already living at 61, Hanover Street, Portsea. His family came originally from Gosport and he was probably born in Portsmouth c.1750. In his youth he was an assistant of Benjamin West's at Windsor and for a few years taught drawing to the younger children of George III before taking up his post at the Naval College where he remained until 1810, thereafter working from his home in the High Street, with spells in London, Winchester and Bath. He died at Southsea and was buried nearby at Wymering in 1826. Livesay was the first local painter of any note, contributing portraits, landscapes, genre and fancy pictures to exhibitions at the Royal Academy although now he is mostly remembered for several studies of naval battles and two large elaborate paintings of military reviews at Hatfield and Portsmouth respectively.

Whatever his limitations as an artist, he was an enterprising man, at least in his early days, quickly recognising the commercial advantages of working closely with engravers to produce cheap widely available versions of works, occasionally publishing them himself, sometimes with his nephew John Livesay, Writing Master at the College (1799–1832), and well known engravers including John Wells and Joseph Constantine Stadler. In June 1798 Richard Livesay produced a series of 'colored views of the Isle of Wight' incorporating regular troops and militia, a series of five engraved as aquatints by Wells for which a combined prospectus and subscription list was issued. A review of the militia at Hatfield by the artist was also sold as an engraved aquatint by Stadler in 1802. Two years later there appeared *French Gun Vessels, Captured Jany 31 1804, by His Majesty's Ships Tribune and Hydra,* also engraved by Stadler. Accuracy and attention to detail were crucial to his work. It was said that the Hatfield painting contained over 5,000 figures, three of which in the lower left hand corner show the back view of three figures, a man sketching (said to be the artist), accompanied by a woman and child. The *Military Review of the Worcestershire Regiment on Southsea Common…14th October 1800,* shows a

18. Richard and John Livesay, *TO GEORGE MONTAGU ESQ ADMIRAL OF THE BLUE AND NAVAL COMMANDER IN CHIEF AT PORTSMOUTH This Print representing the FRENCH GUN VESSELS, Captured Jany 31 1804 by His Majesty's Ships TRIBUNE and HYDRA Commanded by Captains Bennett and Mundy Is Respectfully Inscribed by His Obliged and Most Obedt. Servt. Rd Livesay*. Portsmouth City Museums.

solitary seated man staring at the assembled troops, possibly also the painter [Plate 10]. Betsy Fremantle attended a similar review on the Common by the Dukes of York and Cambridge in August 1803, describing it as, 'a very charming sight' and was particularly struck by the sun tans of a regiment of Dragoons, recently returned from Egypt. Livesay was so pre-occupied in completing the Hatfield picture that he was reprimanded by the Admiralty in June 1801 for outstaying his leave from the Academy in order to complete it. A later and very different work, *Portsmouth Dock Yard Pensions Society* (1820) engraved by Stadler, was perhaps Livesay's final published work with local appeal.

Some indication of the range of his interest emerges from the papers of a former pupil, Richard Baigent, that include a water colour and ink sketch of a cottage in the Isle of Wight (1806), ink and wash drawings of sailing ships (1790), three individual watercolours of an unnamed man, woman and child (n.d.) and several engravings of portraits by the artist. The details of the sale of 61, Hanover Street are far more informative, as the contents included:

'…large and highly finished Paintings of the Royal Family, representing the introduction of the Duchess of York to the Royal Family, containing genuine portraits…with the Royal permission; a very fine picture by Titian. The other pictures are a select collection of highly-finished Landscapes by Mr Livesay, connected with a variety of domestic and fancy pictures, some interesting Naval subjects of victories &c; some very fine drawings, highly finished by Mr Livesay in elegant and valuable frames of large dimensions: Views of Wales, Isle of Wight, and Shipping'.

19. Richard Livesay, *Portsmouth Dock Yard Pensions Society*, 1820. Portsmouth City Museums.

Among the prints on offer were:

> 'a choice collection after the greatest masters, viz Poussin, Rubens, Guido, Reynolds, West, Kauffman and Loutherbourg with a few tinted outlines, equal to drawings of that most interesting view presented from Portsdown hill, looking Southwards; a fine naval print &c…'

John Livesay shared his uncle's concerns for accuracy. He not only assisted him, but worked locally as a drawing master, at Mrs Scarlett's Ladies Seminary, in St George's Square and has been described as a competent painter in his own right. It was not always easy to satisfy demands for information, but in this instance he was obviously doing his best:

'Portsea 17th January 1806

Sir,

Herewith you will receive what Sketches & Remarks I have hitherto been able to collect relative to the Action but which I'm afraid will not be of much Service to you, however such as they are I am very happy in transmitting.

Most of the Ships which are here have been paid off & their crews dispersed on board other Ships & the Ships taken into Dock, they are all dismantled therefore cannot speak as to their loss of Masts so correctly as I could wish The Victory lost her Top Mast & Mizen Mast about the middle of the Action. The Temeraire her Main & Miz. T. Masts.

The whole Fleet fought under White Ensigns The Ships in general had 1 Ensign at the Peak 1 in the Mizn Rigging & a Jack on the F.T. Mast Stay. It does not appear from the Conversations I have had with the Officers that the Combined Fleet was so much in the form of a Crescent as Lord Collingwood mentions in his Letter.

I have sent the Sketch of the Victory which I spoke of in my last the balustrades on the Galleries are not pencilled but in one Corner, but enough to show what the rest should be. If there is any thing in which my Services may be all desireable, I beg Sir, that you will make no Scruple of writing to me as I shall feel myself much honoured thereby.'

It is possible that the marine painter Nicholas Pocock was the unknown recipient of this letter, as it is known that he was in correspondence with Livesay, who provided him with several drawings relating to Trafalgar.

By the time of Richard Livesay's death in 1826 he seems to have been largely forgotten by his contemporaries, the local press dismissing the event in one line. In fact he died in poverty, his nephew and heir John Livesay, renouncing his claims when it became apparent that his late uncle's debts were likely to exceed the value of the estate. Joseph Farington, the gossipy Secretary to the Royal Academy, who invariably sought out local artists on his travels and whose diaries are a major source for this period, fails to mention him, or his successor during two visits to Portsmouth in 1817 and 1818. Perhaps on the first occasion Farington was too preoccupied with his tour of the Dockyard which he took in with an artist's eye:

'We first went to the Observatory & from thence had a fine Panorama view of Portsmouth, – the Dock Yard, Gosport, & the surrounding Sea & Country. – Here I sat some time contemplating the various objects which came into the view – viz – Portsmouth, – Spithead, – Block fort – Hazlar Hospital – Fort Monkton – Gosport, – The Magazine, – the whole of the Dock Yard – The Commissioner's House, a very Handsome stone building with a Court before it & Iron Palisades also the distant Landscape of Ports down – Nelson's Pillar &c.'

When he returned in September 1818, he was taken up with the scandal of the younger Francis Wheatley, who after deserting from the army and an unsuccessful attempt at elopement, came down to Portsmouth:

'and there supported Himself by painting trifling things, & by swindling practices, & He also married a young woman & had 2 children. He then deserted Her & went to London after having by borrowing & swindling raised money enough for His present purpose. The last heard of Him was, that He had used the name of persons at Portsmouth, and by so doing had obtained from them several articles of trade.'

Livesay's successor John Christian Schetky, born in Scotland of an Hungarian father, John, a composer and Maria Reinagle, sister of the artist Joseph Reinagle, was a far livelier character. By the time he succeeded Livesay as what turned out to be the College's final drawing master, for it closed in 1836, he had walked from Paris to Rome where he studied for several months, and had taught drawing at Oxford and Sandhurst. For much of his long life he exhibited at the Royal Academy, one of his final works being the Spithead Review of 1867 occasioned by the visit of the Sultan of Turkey.

In common with his predecessors, Schetky's daily life was not over demanding, if this account of his daily routine written to his future wife, Charlotte Trevenen, is to be believed:

'You wish to know my style and manner of living? Why, faith that's soon said – though perhaps 'twere better not! In the morning I commonly get up before I go anywhere! And that's not very early, which, however, may be accounted for by *early* habits of sitting *late*. I paint till time to go to College: and if I don't dine on board some man-of-war or another I paint after dinner again as long as I can see, as that meal seldom requires more than ten or fifteen minutes: then saunter in my garden chucking the young plants and flowers under the chin, delighted to watch their progress; and while at tea, commonly some friend calls, or I call on some friend living near me – perhaps a hand at cards, or what's more commonly the case, and suits me better, a little music, – what a deal I have got to learn in this heavenly art when you come to lead me! Well, I have an awkward trick of sitting by myself thinking when all the world around me is fast asleep, and then I am slow to rise in the morning. Now my dearest, you have a day of my life, and one is very like another. I am desired not to read at night, and by daylight I have no time, so that I live in happy ignorance. I miss Sir James Gordon, gone to Plymouth, for there I went every evening and made sketches for intended pictures, while he corrected the rigging for me; you know he is a captain in the navy, and now governor of Plymouth Hospital…'

Schetky was popular with the students at the College, breaking convention in taking the more promising for sketching trips up the harbour in the College boat [Plate 11]. They were amused at his dress and habits that gave him 'all the manner and appearance of a sailor' although he had never served in the Royal Navy and impressed at his ability to correct two sketchbooks at a time. It seems he was ambidextrous, a gift that doubtless served him well for his other passion music, and he was the moving spirit in getting up concerts where he and his fellow amateurs 'delighted their friends and themselves by a very excellent performance of the string quartets and other chamber music of Haydn, Beethoven, and dear old Corelli.' On these occasions Schetky was an enthusiastic if erratic performer on the flute and violoncello:

'He seldom practised between – whiles; his instrument frequently arrived at the rehearsals minus one of its strings, or wofully out of tune, and had to be put in order on the spot; he generally played as much from ear as from note; yet his part was always given with a facility of execution, and a perfection of taste and feeling, which would set his hard-working coadjutors railing at the comparatively dry correctness won by their own persevering efforts. "Well, it's in the blood!" was their consolation, when the erratic artist would from time to time produce some of his father's delicately-veined violoncello music or graceful pianoforte sonatas.'

20. John Christian Schetky, *The Arrival of the King of France in Portsmouth Harbour*, 1844. By courtesy of the Witt Library, Courtauld Institute, London.

Following his departure from Portsmouth, Schetky secured a post at the East India College Addiscombe, but as Marine Painter to Queen Victoria he retained close links with Portsmouth and was present at the arrival of King Louis Philippe of France on a state visit in October 1844. This letter from the painter to his daughter captures both the atmosphere of the occasion and his approach to painting it. He had got up at six o'clock, crossed the harbour to Blockhouse Fort, ready to sketch the approaching vessel:

> 'It was very cold and misty, and I could see nothing except many boats pulling out to meet the illustrious visitor; so after standing there on the beach all alone for some time (like a fool!) I went back to a comfortable breakfast at my hotel (The Quebec). Then about nine o'clock The cry was 'He's coming'. I instantly returned to my post, and made my first sketch of his distant appearance – another just as he entered the harbour – and another as he was passing up to the moorings, where his Majesty's ship was made fast. I then went on board the royal yacht Victoria and Albert, and sketched during the day; and as we lay near the Gomer (the French royal yacht), I had a good view of all that passed – thousands of boats round the ship, all having flags and all cheering like madmen. And when Prince Albert with the Duke of Wellington came in the royal barge to go on board and welcome the King, the *yell* of delight was overpowering.'

Much of this mixture of formality and popular excitement is captured in the resulting composition, *Arrival of the King of France in Portsmouth Harbour* (1844), the French yacht hemmed in by the crowds of sightseers in boats large and small, his grasp of the situation impressive, and like much of his work well crafted.

Nothing contrasts more sharply than Turner's interpretation of the same event [Plate 12]. The painter had known Louis Philippe during his years of exile in England, and in 1838 the King had presented him with a jewelled gold snuff box in return for a copy of *Picturesque Views in England and Wales*. Turner was in the neighbourhood and witnessed the King's arrival. The two resulting paintings were for many years thought to be Venetian scenes belonging to the 1840s, but recent research suggests otherwise: the size of the canvasses, the grey tones of the sky, and the red uniforms of the soldiers, together with other contemporary descriptions of the occasion, reinforce this conclusion. But in Turner's work it is not any of this that matters, for his major concern, particularly in his later years, was to capture the ever changing characteristics of light and colour, factors that transcend location, in a way that earlier works do not. As a contemporary remarked, of an engraving of the painter's *St Mark's Place, Venice* (1842), 'The picture was not meant to be topographically correct, but to be a beautiful dream, true in the feeling it conveyed.' It is re-assuring to know that whatever each thought of the other's work, Schetky and Turner had been friends since 1818 when Turner visited his brother and sister in Edinburgh. This friendship extended to practical collaboration, for in 1823 Schetky loaned Turner several sketches, when the latter was engaged in painting his version of the battle of Trafalgar. Such behaviour was by no means unusual, for in 1838/9, Clarkson Stanfield painted the sky in Schetky's *Loss of the Royal George*, while much earlier c.1774, Thomas Jones was responsible for most of Paton's *View of Portsmouth from Portsdown Hill*.

Society was quick to take up drawing, often combined with painting in watercolours and by the late eighteenth century it was regarded as a polite accomplishment in both sexes. Caroline Wilkinson of Portchester began drawing in 1820. Her *Journal* includes a visit to the Isle of Wight and mentions 'sketching the chine & adjacent rocks at Blackgang' and 'the gate by which you enter' at Carisbrooke Castle. The Reverend John Skinner included nine watercolour sketches of Portsmouth and its approaches in his *Journal* (1831), beginning with embarkation of himself and his family at Yarmouth when he drew:

> 'the Pilot of our Vessel, Mr Dore, who is by no means adorable if we regard his face only, and his figure, but I doubt not he is every way qualified for his employ'. Vide Sketch 3. No 6, describes the first view of Portsmouth lying equal to the water's edge. No.7, the fleet off St Helen's. No.8 is a near view of Portsmouth and the strong fortresses which guard the approach to this celebrated naval station. No.9 Portchester Castle.'

Having disembarked from the steamer, the party made their way to the George in the High Street, strolled about the fortifications 'under the shade of lofty Elm trees', returned to the Point, where they hired a boat and were rowed around the harbour, ending their visit with a tour of the Royal yacht. A few years later (1839), a young lady, whose name is now lost, made a similar journey from the Isle of Wight. Following a walk to the King's Rooms, and a look out to Spithead at the attempts made in that year to raise the *Royal George*, she returned to the Quebec Hotel, stopping on the way to draw some men boring a well, and spent the rest of evening with her family, looking at the ships as they sailed in and out of the harbour.

It was not unusual for artists to combine painting, drawing and teaching to gain a livelihood When Livesay retired he moved to the High Street, where he advertised for pupils, describing himself as 'portrait and landscape painter' teaching drawing by the 'R.A. Method' and continued to work at Mr Neave's Academy at his old home in Portsea. Another local contemporary, John Lane, taught 'Figures, Landscapes and Perspectives on the easiest principles' and a third, 'Mr Penley,' offered tuition in 'all

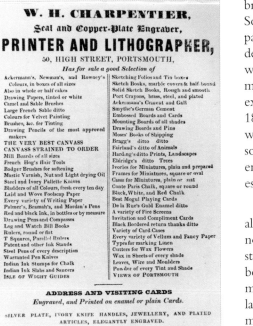

W. H. CHARPENTIER,

Seal and Copper-Plate Engraver,

PRINTER AND LITHOGRAPHER,

50, HIGH STREET, PORTSMOUTH,

Has for sale a good Selection of

Ackermann's, Newman's, and Rowney's Colours, in boxes of all sizes	Sketching Folios and Tin boxes
Also in whole or half cakes	Sketch Books, marble covers & half-bound
Drawing Papers, tinted or white	Solid Sketch Books, Rough and smooth
Camel and Sable Brushes	Port Crayons, brass, steel, and plated
Large French Sable ditto	Ackermann's Cement and Gall
Colours for Velvet Painting	Smythe's German Cement
Brushes, &c. for Tinting	Embossed Boards and Cards
Drawing Pencils of the most approved makers	Mounting Boards of all shades
THE VERY BEST CANVASS	Drawing Boards and Pins
CANVASS STRAINED TO ORDER	Moses' Books of Shipping
Mill Boards of all sizes	Bragg's ditto ditto
French Hog's Hair Tools	Fairland's ditto of Animals
Badger Brushes for softening	Harding's ditto Prints, Landscapes
Mastic Varnish, Nut and Light drying Oil	Eldridge's ditto Trees
Steel and Ivory Pallette Knives	Ivories for Miniatures, plain and prepared
Bladders of all Colours, fresh every ten day	Frames for Miniatures, square or oval
Laid and Wove Foolscap Paper	Cases for Miniatures, plain or mat
Every variety of Writing Paper	Conte Paris Chalk, square or round
Palmer's, Bramah's, and Mordan's Pens	Black, White, and Red Chalk
Red and black Ink, in bottles or by measure	Best Mogul Playing Cards
Drawing Pens and Compasses	De la Rue's Gold Enamel ditto
Log and Watch Bill Books	A variety of Fire Screens
Rulers, round or flat	Invitation and Compliment Cards
T Squares, Parallel Rulers	Black Bordered return thanks ditto
Patent and other Ink Stands	Variety of Card Cases
Steel Pens of every description	Every variety of Vellum and Fancy Paper
Warranted Pen Knives	Types for marking Linen
Indian Ink Stumps for Chalk	Cutters for Wax Flowers
Indian Ink Slabs and Saucers	Wax in Sheets of every shade
ISLE OF WIGHT GUIDES	Leaves, Wire and Moulders
	Powder of every Tint and Shade
	VIEWS OF PORTSMOUTH

ADDRESS AND VISITING CARDS

Engraved, and Printed on enamel or plain Cards.

SILVER PLATE, IVORY KNIFE HANDLES, JEWELLERY, AND PLATED ARTICLES, ELEGANTLY ENGRAVED.

Mourning Rings and Brooches Engraved.

SPOONS, FORKS, &c. ERASED, AND RE-ENGRAVED.

☞ *Views, Plans of Estates, Circular Letters, &c. Lithographed.*

21. *Goods Sold by W.H. Charpentier*, 1837. Portsmouth City Council Library Service.

branches of drawing' at his academy, 12, King's Terrace, Southsea, as well as 'miniature, landscape and flower painting &c in Oils or Water Colours.' Richard Poate described himself as 'late Senior Pupil of Mr Penley' when he set up as a miniature painter and drawing master in 1829 at his academy 9, King Street, Portsea, exhibiting at the Royal Academy between 1845 and 1869. It is perhaps fitting that his final working address was in Pembroke Road, where apart from tuition, he sold artists' materials, oleographs, photographs and engravings, only several doors away from the newly established School of Science and Art.

Regardless of their circumstances, artists and public alike, made use of a growing number of local booksellers, not only for artists' materials, but for engravings, stationery, books and other publications. Many of the booksellers were also printers and publishers. The two most prestigious in Portsmouth were Comerfords, in the late eighteenth century, followed by Charpentier's, who moved from Portsea to the High Street in 1827. William Henry Charpentier sold lithographs, drawings, artists' materials and also published a series of guidebooks, commissioning James Calcott to draw as a frontispiece, *The King's Promenade Rooms & Baths, Southsea Beach* for the guide of 1837.

22. F.M. Shepherd, *High Street, Portsmouth*, 1840. Portsmouth City Museums.

23. J. Harwood, *Southsea*, 1841. Portsmouth City Museums.

In his summer tour of 1774, Gilpin enthused over the view from Portsdown Hill across Portsea Island describing it (with pardonable exaggeration) as 'grander in its kind than any part of the globe can exhibit,' an opinion echoed by William Daniell, another talented exponent of the picturesque, in 1822, as a 'prospect…surpassing for its grandeur and variety'. The qualities that Gilpin and his followers praised in a landscape were 'ruggedness of texture, singularity, variety, irregularity and the power to stimulate imagination.' The last point is perhaps the most important as it proved a convenient bridge between the picturesque and the romantic, a way of looking that the painter hoped to induce or share with the viewer, demonstrated in works by J.M.W. Turner and Clarkson Stanfield for several publications devoted to coastal scenery published between 1810 and 1838, in which Portsmouth harbour featured. Stanfield argued forcibly that art could appeal to the feelings without sacrificing 'the accuracy of truth with all the poetry of effect.' It is perhaps worth remembering he was for some years a successful designer and painter of theatrical scenery, abilities that served him well as an artist [Plate 13]. Both painters fed a growing enthusiasm for tourism more widely encouraged by the publication of large numbers of steel engravings on topographical and architectural subjects in the 1840s, the work of London based firms such as Harwood, Robinson, and Rock & Co, many of which ended up in scrapbooks, a pleasing record of family holidays. Turner himself was a frequent visitor to Portsmouth, from 1801 hoping to catch the return of Danish ships taken after Copenhagen, 1814 during the celebrations of victory over Napoleon, in 1844 whilst staying on the Isle of Wight, and lastly in 1849, as part of his *Antiquarian and Picturesque Tour Round the Southern Coast of England.*

Edward William Cooke had a great love of the sea and ships, and as a young man was closely influenced by Stanfield, who was also a family friend. He grew up with an appreciation of the English topographical tradition as his father George Cooke engraved and published works in this field, including views of London. Cooke had a precocious talent and at the age of 17 journeyed to

24. E.W. Cooke, *View from the Saluting Platform*, c.1836. Portsmouth City Museums.

Portsmouth, chaperoned by his grandfather, in search of new subjects for *Fifty Plates of Shipping and Craft,* that appeared in 12 parts between 1828 and 1831. There is a freshness and spontaneity in the artist's description of the harbour, in this diary entry 5th June 1828:

> 'We next entered the Port (now comes the treat) that fine ship the *Victory*…extended her huge sheer across the Harbour and contrasted well with the minor craft around such as Colliers, Sloops, wherries &c the other men of war lying up in Ordinary – the Hulks – Prison Ships – Navy cutters – Pilot boats – Luggers – Steamers – dredgers, mooring lighters &c &c altogether presented a most novel and interesting appearance. The immense ranges of building in and connected with the Royal Dock Yard formed the background and finished a very beautiful picture. So much for a first glance of P. – in returning from the Steamer I looked out for a good house wherein to rest my Hide and soon Prog'd one with a circular stern which overlooked the harbour. Here we went and found it was the Still Tavern, situate at the Point, at the entrance of the Port …After a safe Anchorage & a good laying in of Provisions, we retired to our Hammocks & enjoyed a comfortable share of balmy sleep.'

He met Schetky who 'was very much pleased with the Numbers of *Shipping*. Said it was the <u>most correct</u> work of the kind he had seen and no doubt he should give me some commissions. He wished to show them to the Governor and Admiral of this Port so I left them.' But more was to follow:

25. E.W. Cooke, *Gosport, Flagship Saluting*, c.1836. Portsmouth City Museums.

'We went (in a wherry) over the Harbour to Gosport. Fine view of the *Victory* began to sketch it. Had not done much when I looked at my watch – it was ½ p 6 and the post goes out at 7, no time to be lost so we leap't in a boat & back we came again to the Point. Just had time to scrubb up my letter, gallop'd off & got it to the box in time. Then I wished myself back at Gosport but it was too late.'

The same relentless pace characterised a further visit in 1831, concluding on a similarly upbeat note:

'July 1st...Met F[rank] W[aring] at the baths & had a cruize with him to Spithead & ret, to tea At the Still at 9.0. Met him at the Assembly Rooms, heard music, won a bottle of Eau de Cologne at a raffle. Glorious fine day.'

Some of Cooke's early work was published in E & W Findon's *Ports Harbours & Watering Places* (1836) including *View from the Saluting Platform* and *Gosport, Flagship Saluting* both showing a well developed knowledge of ships and rigging, part of the secret of his success in a long career as a marine painter.

CHAPTER 4

LOCAL ARTISTS
AND EARLY EXHIBITIONS

26. James Calcott, *The King's Promenade Rooms & Baths, Southsea Beach*, 1837. Portsmouth City Council Library Service.

The emergence of Southsea and its burgeoning reputation as a watering place in the 1820s and '30s marks a new phase in the history of Portsmouth. It was not just the return of peace in 1815 or the widening popularity of sea bathing that encouraged visitors and induced a number of 'genteel families to settle in the town or nearby', but improved facilities such as the King's Rooms 'a handsome library, reading room and baths' built by Henry Hollingsworth, property speculator and publisher/author of the *Portsmouth Guide* (1822) that advertised the attractions of the place. Summer amusements listed here and in W.H. Charpentier's, *The New Portsmouth Guide* (1837) included watching military man-oeuvres on Southsea Common, cricket, and a recently established annual rowing regatta, where:

> 'hundreds, or rather thousands of vessels and boats of all sizes, from the fishing punt to the princely yacht, are seen as it were covering the face of the water with animation: Whilst tens of thousands of genteely dressed persons line the ramparts and beach where they enjoy this truly national fete'.

27. J. Harwood, *Southsea Terrace*, 1847. Portsmouth City Museums.

In August 1848, the Queen attended, although it was 'very cold and raining…and gave away the prizes to the boatmen.' But musical and ceremonial events associated with the garrison and port, gave Portsmouth its distinctive flavour, if Henry Alford is to be believed:

> 'There are some very good military bands here, and they play on the fortifications every night at nine o'clock till nearly ten. The music is very fine …Every morning at daybreak they fire a gun from the walls which is answered by the ships in the harbour. In the evening at sunset they fire another, and another at nine o'clock, then the various bands strike up, and play on different parts of the walls till nearly ten, when they play "God save the King" and stop.'

The trooping of the Town Guard on Governor's Green during the summer and autumn months was an additional attraction in the 1860s:

> 'This, to the stranger, a most pleasing sight, and usually attracts a large crowd of elegantly dressed people. On this beautiful field, the regimental bands of the garrison perform select pieces of music during the season, notice of which is given in programmes issued weekly.'

To the existing diversions provided by shipping, were added tours of the royal yacht and of more long term significance, Nelson's *Victory*. The coming of the railway in 1847 increased the scope for excursions not just to Netley, but the New Forest and beyond, in turn encouraging further growth of Southsea, much of it the brainchild of the architect and developer Thomas Ellis Owen, between 1835 and 1860.

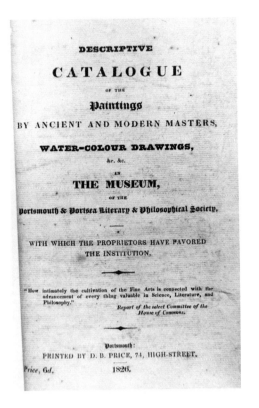

DESCRIPTIVE

CATALOGUE

OF THE

Paintings

BY ANCIENT AND MODERN MASTERS,

WATER-COLOUR DRAWINGS,

&c. &c.

IN

THE MUSEUM,

OF THE

Portsmouth & Portsea Literary & Philosophical Society,

WITH WHICH THE PROPRIETORS HAVE FAVORED
THE INSTITUTION.

"How intimately the cultivation of the Fine Arts is connected with the
advancement of every thing valuable in Science, Literature, and
Philosophy."
*Report of the select Committee of the
House of Commons.*

Portsmouth:
PRINTED BY D. B. PRICE, 74, HIGH-STREET.

Price, 6d. 1826.

28. Anon, *Portsmouth & Portsea Literary and Philosophical Society Exhibition Catalogue* (Front cover), 1826. Portsmouth City Council Library Service.

All these factors to varying degrees contributed to a growing interest in the arts leading to the establishment of the Portsmouth and Portsea Literary and Philosophical Society (1815), under whose auspices a public exhibition, the first of its kind, took place at the Society's museum in Pembroke Road between July and September 1826. By May:

'Many offers of pictures, and other subjects…have already been most liberally made by individuals in the towns and neighbourhood, and we have no doubt but the proposed measure will not only prove highly interesting, but be advantageous to our resident artists, by affording an opportunity for bringing before the public the productions of their periods.'

The prospectus stated that in addition to oils, watercolours, drawings and engravings, statues, coins and medals were to be included. Owners, mostly professional men living in the town, were expected to provide descriptions of their exhibits, as well as making it clear whether or not they were for sale. The catalogue shows that interest in painting was not confined to old masters (although they were in the majority), but to contemporaries also, revealing a growing interest in modern art amongst the middle classes and rather different values from more traditional patrons:

'These rough and ready customers wanted interesting subjects; variety, resemblance to nature, genuiness of the article, and fresh paint; they had no ancestors as founders of galleries it was necessary to consult; no critical gentlemen and writers of valuable books to snub them when they were in spirits; nothing to lead them by the nose except their own shrewdness, their own interests, their own tastes…'

Old masters, engravings and watercolours were hung alongside modern works, some on loan, which was not unusual at this time. Six locally based painters exhibited, their work closely scrutinised in the press:

'Mr Gilbert of Chichester has a splendid landscape full of repose and beauty, with many other smaller productions which do him high credit… Mr W. Dashwood has some pleasing views in the Isle of Wight, as has also Mr Thomas; while Mr Lane, the Curator of the Institution, and under whose immediate care the whole of the gallery has been arranged, has contributed a large subject 'The Descent from the Cross', and several highly spirited portraits of individuals in the neighbourhood. Besides these, there are many specimens of water colour drawings, some fine marine pictures &c. We repeat, that it is an exhibition most creditable to those by whom it has been fostered, to the Institution in whose rooms it is displayed, and to the town in general.'

29. George Cole, *Cato, the Property of the Rt. Hon. Sir Robert Peel Bart., sketched at Drayton, July 4th 1845*. Portsmouth City Museums.

Lane had once been a fencing instructor at the College. Dashwood and Thomas were naval officers. Gilbert had some years previously moved from Portsmouth to Chichester. It is also interesting that works by Livesay, Elliott (another naval officer with local connections) and Northcote's pupil William Salter were on view and that Schetky lent a painting from his own collection, as well as showing two of his own works. History paintings, battle and literary subjects dominated the exhibition. At Plymouth a comparable town in many respects, a similar event in the 1820s revealed a taste for landscape and architectural subjects, while portraiture and marine painting were poorly represented in each. Yet it is to the credit of both that they were among the 14 or so other provincial towns holding public exhibitions between 1810 and 1830.

The 1826 exhibition demonstrated that there was enough local support to sustain a small but growing number of artists. The most interesting of these was George Cole who reputedly began his career as a ship's painter, was self taught at least in his early days, and who initially made his reputation as an animal painter, advertising his skills through 'the splendidly painted though necessarily exaggerated canvasses with which the outside of [Wombwell's travelling menagerie] was adorned' at the annual Free Mart Fair. In his Portsmouth days Cole experimented with various art forms from still life to animal painting and portraiture before emerging as a landscape painter, and was largely influenced by the Dutch and Norwich schools whose work he saw as he visited country houses in search of commissions to paint horses and other animals. Among his early patrons were the Rev. Sir John Barker-Mill, Bart., of Mottisfont Abbey, General Codrington, and the Peel family. But it is also clear from details in his studio sale of 1852 that he was painting landscapes in the neighbourhood at Cosham, Southwick and further afield, Kingley Vale and Bramshott. The impressive oil, *London Road, Portsdown Hill* (1867), is a copy of number 69 in the catalogue, in which about 20 can be identified as the work of this artist. His eldest son Vicat Cole, also a landscape painter, had 10 works mostly landscapes included in the same sale, that included paintings by their associate George Shalders, the son of an actor at the Portsmouth Theatre [Plate 14].

In 1855 the Literary and Philosophical Society decided to hold its own exhibition and appealed for 'loans of pictures or articles of virtu' from 'the Ladies and Gentlemen of Portsmouth and the Neighbourhood'. Some 150 pictures were displayed at the Society's museum along with copies of 13 watercolours from the Queen's collection, 'and four Steroscopes, with a great variety of slides, by the London Steroscopic Company', and 'several interesting figures and statuettes in Bronze, Parian, and Terra Cotta, lent by Messrs. Emanuel and Mr Hudson.' On this occasion the dominant role of local

30. Anon, *Portsmouth & Portsea Literary and Philosophical Society – The Institute*, 1831. Portsmouth City Records Office.

artists was far more apparent, their appeal seemingly to lie mainly in the didactic, anecdotal character of the works under discussion, if the unknown correspondent in the *Hampshire Telegraph* is to be believed, for want of a surviving catalogue:

'There are several pictures by G. Cole, who resided amongst us for years, and is now resident in London. It is not necessary to enlarge upon the merits of his pictures. There are several painted in his happiest style. Our townsman, Mr Poate has produced several pictures which reflect the highest credit upon him. His "Sailors' Home" appropriately dedicated to Captain Hall and the Officers of the Royal Navy, is a very excellent painting. The artist thoroughly enters into the subject, – we have the fun and frolic, as well as the attendant evils of the old places of resort, contrasted with the order and propriety, – and the elements of knowledge and improvement which surround the sailors in the Home provided for them. The merchant sailor in the foreground, unpacking relics from the Crimea, proclaims that the Home is open to men of both services. The group discussing the merits of a plan of some naval engagement is well conceived. We repeat that the picture, apart from the excellent character of the painting, indicates that the artist is thoroughly conversant with the habits of that portion of the population, which frequents the localities he has depicted…"The Sailor's Return", the property of Mr W Collins, is another picture by the same artist, and in general its character and tone is excellent…Mr Cunliffe is particularly happy in his "Cat and Partridges." The "Sortie at Jallalabad" is a picture which demands study: it is an historical picture: the details were taken from the descriptions of eyewitnesses. The grouping is excellent, and many of the figures are represented in the most spirited manner: a great deal of labour has been bestowed upon it…Mr Shalders, another townsman, is well represented. His landscapes are very clever productions…'

Yet whatever local painters did, it was the overall character of the town that continued to draw visitors, to what Lewis's *Illustrated Handbook of* Portsmouth (1860) described as 'the chief Naval arsenal in the World'. At a time of growing patriotic sentiment in the aftermath of the Crimean War when Anglo French tensions were running high, the author claimed:

> '…The Common – The docks – the Fortifications – the very Hotels and some of the private dwellings, are so many chronicles, bringing before the mind's eye stirring events – events that remind an Englishman that Portsmouth has sheltered host after host of warriors, and sent them forth to do battle for their country and liberty – men whose name is legion, but whose glorious lives and example make us feel that we are treading upon a soil that has been for ages part of the marrow bone of England.'

Indeed, 'the subtle views' and 'novelties seawards' continued to capture their imagination: shipping, including reviews of the fleet, the harbour, Dockyard, fortifications, the High Street and its neighbour-hood. Sir Charles Oman's childhood memories of Southsea in 1864 included the 53rd [Regiment], 'marching with their band to the Garrison Church on Sunday, and of the curious scraping noise which their bayonets made against the seats, when they stood up or sat down at various points in the service.' The youthful George Eaton, on a painting holiday in the locality with his family, was also impressed by the military aspects of the town [Plate 15]:

'There are an immense number of soldiers in Portsmouth and you are constantly seeing them march about the streets…At tea time I went to the guard room at the saluting battery where the soldiers were drawn up and some drummers were playing but it was all over when I got there. After our walk – (after tea) William and I walked up the High Street with many other people to hear the drummers play as they marched quickly up to another guard room – They played splendidly. The drums rattled like guns.'

Among the local artists who respond-ed to this theme were the little known David Cunliffe, some of whose sketches of soldiers exercising on the Common have survived, and Richard Poate, former Drawing Master at Addiscombe Military College and at Woolwich, who was com-missioned to paint the civic banquet held

31. David Cunliffe, *Soldier at Musket Drill*, c.1840. Portsmouth City Museums.

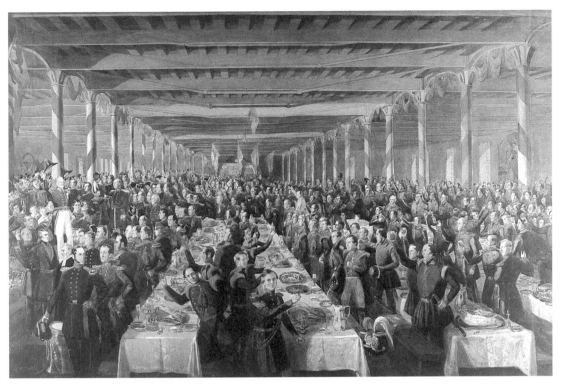

32. R.H.C. Ubsdell, *Rear Admiral Prescott C.B. proposing to the Royal Dock Yard Batn. The Health of Her Majesty the Queen, May 25 1848*. Portsmouth City Museums.

on Governor's Green, a lavish entertainment for naval and military personnel on 16th September 1856 given to the 2,300 soldiers, sailors and marines returning from the Crimean War. Several hundred guests are shown in the temporary pavilion built for the occasion, on a raised platform or balcony. Naval ratings occupy the table on the left, with infantry at the lower end and all the table next to this. The pavilion is decorated with flags of the allies, while the crest of Portsmouth can be seen in the top left of the painting. The figure on the lower right is believed to be Dr Engledue of Portsmouth, one of the chief sponsors of the event [Plate 16]. The picture is comparable to R.H.C. Ubsdells's study of the Portsmouth Volunteer Dockyard Battalion, painted in 1848, for its attention to the faces (individual portraits?) of many of the volunteers who are shown seated at long tables, in what appears to be a large storeroom or boathouse, and are being addressed by Admiral Prescott, who is proposing a toast to the Queen. Like a later portrayal of the volunteer cavalry exercising on Portsdown Hill by the same artist, these paintings tell us much about contemporary preoccupations. The guidebooks of the 1860s and '70s also brought out the character of the town, Abel Hayward commending the military bands that could be heard on Clarence Pier, as well as 'the frequent military displays and visits of vessels of war, not only of England, but of other countries, giv(ing) a liveliness unequalled'. Hayward's *Guide* (1876?), echoed these sentiments and was also complimentary about the Esplanade, noting that 'A Ladies Mile for horse exercise is contemplated' and is probably the earliest authority to praise the quality of the shops in King's Road and Palmerston Road.

33. Anon, *Naval Review at Spithead in Honour of the Sultan of Turkey*, 1867. Portsmouth City Museums.

The most important naval review of these years took place in 1867, part of the state visit of Abdul Aziz, Sultan of Turkey. The painter, Robert Leslie, whose interest in sailing frequently brought him to Portsmouth, was an eyewitness, and in this account reveals something of the hurry, bustle and excitement of the occasion, since he had an invitation to see the review from the *Achilles*, where his son was a midshipman:

> 'To be in time for the boat…I had to take the last train from Southampton the night before, which arrived at Portsmouth soon after midnight, where, in company with many others I spent an hour or two before daybreak in the railway-station; after which, refreshed by a cup of coffee, I strolled down to Southsea beach. It was a dirty, fresh, blowing morning, and soon after 6 a.m., seeing a boat leave the *Achilles*, I walked back through Point Gate to a sally-port, where I found, even at this early hour, a crowd of elaborately dressed ladies and gentlemen, all waiting for boats from the respective ships named in their cards of invitation…And as one after another the ships' boats dashed in, the wet, shiny oil-skins of their crews contrasted curiously with the summer toilets of the assembled "sisters, cousins and aunts." The water in front of the quay was now a mere jumble of heaving, rolling steam-launches, ships cutters, and smart gigs – reminding one of a crowded street blocked with gentlemen's carriages near one of the great London theatres or the Opera, – only in place of the names or titles of the owners of carriages, it was the name of the man-of-war, to which each boat belonged that was called out by the party waiting for her.'

The event itself was something of an anticlimax, because of the bad weather, 'none of the ships moved that day, so the review was merely a procession of the Royal yacht, the Admiralty yacht and others, up and down between [the two lines] of men-of-war.' In addition the unfortunate Sultan was repeatedly forced to go below deck to be seasick.

If any one picture (a lithograph to be precise) epitomises the optimism of the 1860s, it is surely A. Pernet's *Southsea Common* (1863) with its soldiers on the Common against the backdrop of

34. A. Pernet, *Southsea Common*, c.1863. Portsmouth City Museums.

Southsea's terraces, and in the foreground, Clarence Pier, the esplanade thronged with people, and nearest to the spectator sailing boats and larger steam powered pleasure craft, a commercial work advertising the town and its amenities, proclaiming in bold type at the base that Southsea is 'The Healthiest Spot in England.'

Romanticism in art heightened the appeal of historical subjects to the Victorians, nor was this confined to great victories on land or sea, for there were patriotic lessons to be drawn even from defeat and disaster, if the artist approached the subject in the right spirit with sufficient knowledge. The life of Nelson captured the imagination of artists and public alike, and to a lesser degree so did the loss of the *Royal George* at Spithead with most of her crew on 29th August 1782. A sketch by Rowlandson who visited the spot, shows the masts of the unfortunate ship protruding above the water, where they remained visible for many years to come. Others sought to reconstruct the event in paintings, including Viscount Duncannon (whose work was published by the engraver William Birch in 1789), and Thomas Buttersworth (1800). Later in the 1830s, when a final attempt was made at 'removing the vessel' followed by the destruction of all that was impossible to salvage, William Mitchell, a prolific ship painter, engraved 'the *Sinking of HMS Royal George*…in 1839' based on a drawing in the possession of a local historian, Henry Slight, included with an account of the whole episode, published in 1841. Another publisher, Samuel Horsey of Portsea, also produced an engraved version of the disaster. The town's guidebooks continued to make much of the tragedy, nor were certain other inhabitants slow to profit from it. George Eaton confided to his diary that, 'in Broad Street…we saw in a shop several relics of the *Royal George* & My aunt gave me a book about the sinking & bound in the wood of the wreck.' Schetky's imagination was also sufficiently stirred by the fate of the ship, to take trouble to seek out and interview the few remaining survivors, exhibiting the picture (now at the Tate Gallery, but in very poor condition), at the Royal Academy in 1840:

> 'Being engaged painting a picture descriptive of the event, some 23 years ago, and anxious to get all the information I could for my subject, I went about in yellow-painted post-chaises wherever I heard of any survivors of the melancholy accident – and found an intelligent old gentleman

35. S. Horsey Junr., *Sinking of H.M.S. 'Royal George' at Spithead Aug.29 1782*, c.1840. Portsmouth City Museums.

[William Lawrence] at Morden College on Blackheath – who was then purser's clerk; he answered many of my questions, but, getting much excited – said – "I cannot remember any more but – there was a small craft-tender to the "George", made fast to the buoy of our anchor – and I went with some twenty of the crew and the 4th Lieutenant in the little craft to draw stores from the dockyard at Portsmouth; we had no sooner shoved off in one of the ship's cutters to go on board the tender, than the young Middy of the boat found he had forgot his dirk; the Lieutenant gave the poor boy a wigging for his pains, but we put back that he might get his dirk – the fatal dirk – and as the ship was lying almost on her beam ends – jump'd aboard at one of the lower ports – but unfortunately was longer about getting it than the Lieutenant's patience could contain – and he ordered the boat to shove off – and the dear boy went to the bottom with all hands! (he was the Captain's son, Captain Waghorn).

When we got to the tender the Lieutenant was first on board – and just as I got on deck I heard him say – with an oath – the "George" is going down! I look'd round and saw the last of her!! But I saw no more for my eyes were full of water which I could not stop".'

A more nostalgic attitude towards the past was also hastened by the coming of the steamship and the railway. Their effect on Portsmouth together with dockyard expansion and the destruction of old buildings was not always welcome. In 1849 Turner enthused over the Floating Bridge between Portsmouth and Gosport, describing the mechanism in considerable detail:

'The floating-bridge consists of a large flat-bottomed boat, similar to the busses of the middle ages. The deck is covered with road-stuff, so that carriages drive on board, the same as if it were a continuation of the road itself. This massive vessel plies between two chains, stretched parallel to each other, from one shore to the other. On each side of the vessel are three wheels, that in the centre being of a large diameter. The chains are conducted over the large and under the small wheels, the links fitting into notched grooves on their surface. The large wheel is propelled by steam; the use of the small wheels is to keep the floating mass steady. When the bridge is at either side, the chain, of course, sinks to the bottom, and offers no bar to navigation. Besides standing for carriages and horses, the bridge has a commodious room for the accommodation of passengers. A similar bridge is at Southampton, and another propelled by manual labour, instead of steam, crosses the Arun, at Little Hampton.'

But many of his contemporaries expressed their distaste for modern improvements in no uncertain terms. The painter Alfred Dawson was certainly not alone in complaining about the impact of the new harbour station a few years later:

'How very lively and moving was the old style when there were no ironclads,
And the horrid railway station and sidings on its row of iron sticks did not go
Right across the view.'

The destruction of old buildings reached a climax in the 1870s. Fortunately R.H.C. Ubsdell recorded many that had already disappeared in a number of sketches and watercolours for Sir Frederic Madden's projected history of his native town, a typical example, *View of Government House*, in a letter to his patron, dated 19th October 1840. Madden was not the easiest of men, often criticising Ubsdell for inaccuracies, or grumbling at the expense:

'The prices affixed to Some of the articles are perhaps rather more than I had expected, but you probably have lost much time in doing them. The Old Telegraph I liked very much, as also the Government House & Theatre. The interior of the Chapel, is, I think hardly finished enough, and I should have preferred some figures in the foreground. The next time you come to London, you will be able perhaps to improve it. I send you the half of a 10£ note in this, and for Security Sake have sent the remaining half by todays post to my Sister. If you will call on her I have desired her to give it to you, and I would thank you to pay the balance 1. 2. 0. into her hands, together with an acknowledgement of the receipt of £8.18.0. I have already got all the engravings on letter paper published by

36. R.H.C. Ubsdell, *View of Government House, 1840, in a letter to Sir Frederic Madden, 8 July 1840*. Portsmouth City Records Office.

37. Robert Leslie, *Sketch of a Portsmouth Wherry*, c.1860. © National Maritime Museum, Greenwich, London.

Harward among which are the view of Portsmouth & Bar Gate Southampton you Sent me. I have also drawings of the corporation Plate tolerably accurate, done many years since. For the present therefore I do not wish you to copy anything more for me, as it is not impossible I may be at Portsmouth in the course of next year and can then give further directions, if I judge necessary. The <u>White House</u> appears very like, and I recollect it well.'

However, it is thanks to both men that many buildings lost in these years were recorded.

Robert Leslie mourned the disappearance of the traditional wherries, that plied their trade in the harbour, shown to some effect in William Smyth's *On the Point, Portsmouth* (1857) [Plate 17], but drawn and described in greater detail by Leslie:

'Most of these old passenger wherries are ornamented about the top-streak inside with small notched and incised carvings something in the same way that old country waggons are, and like them are also decorated with certain florid paintings about the board that forms the back of the stern seat. Here, in old times, one often saw tastefully combined with the words "for hire" and the owner's name the portrait of some well-known naval or military hero. I remember when the Princess Victoria was the favourite, surrounded with a confused circle of vegetation, which the owner of the boat would lovingly describe as "Hingland's rose, him braced by the prickly thistle of Scotland backed hup by the Shamrock of the sister hile".'

The decline of the wherries was underlined by the type of passengers they now carried:

'the majority…were drovers, gipsies, pedlars, poachers, tramps, tinkers, half-drunken sailors and soldiers, and their companions. Such fares often required [Peter], the owner's assistance to get not only themselves on board his wherry, but any trifle they had with them, such as a knife-grinder's barrow, a punch's show, or a barrel organ; not to mention live calves, sheep, or pigs, barrels of beer, a few sacks of corn or coal, a plough, dogs and their kennels, live poultry etc, etc.'

The disappearance of these traditional vessels, together with the other dramatic changes of these years were well summed up by the novelist Sir Walter Besant who wrote sadly:

'Now…everything is changed. All the romance went out of the place when they swept away the walls and filled up the moats. The harbour, too, is not what it was: they have wantonly broken up and destroyed nearly all the old historic ships, save the one where Nelson died. Only a few of the venerable hulks remain.'

1864 to 1876 were the years covered by the 'great extension' to the Dockyard, the yard itself trebling in size from 99 to 261 acres, only half of which was land reclaimed from the harbour. The ancient landward fortifications were demolished in the 1870s, to be replaced by 12 forts stretching from Gosport to Portsdown Hill, and together with the new forts in the harbour were known as Palmerston's Follies, after the prime minister responsible for them.

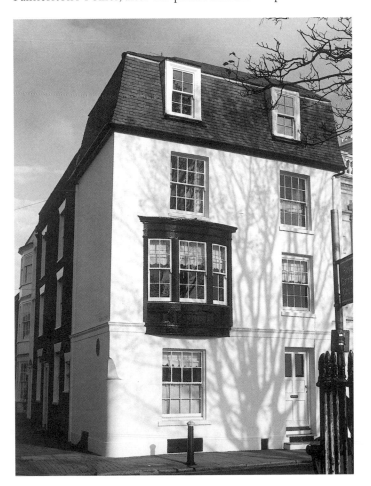

38. Garrick Palmer, *George Cole's House, 1, Green Row (now Pembroke Road), 2004.* © Garrick Palmer.

So ends the first important period of painting in Portsmouth's history, when local artists first appear in significant numbers. It could be argued that a tradition of marine painting fostered by the drawing masters at the naval college, survived its closure in 1836, while a growing interest in art was sustained by the Literary and Philosophical Society through the exhibitions of 1826 and 1855, until its demise in 1860. But Portsmouth was unable to provide sufficient rewards for the more able or ambitious artists. Even a painter with a growing reputation such as George Cole had problems in making a livelihood. The *Hampshire Telegraph* report of a visit to his studio in October 1849 stated that a committee of the artist's friends had drawn up a scheme similar to that of the highly successful Art Union,

39. Anon, *Catalogue of George Cole's Sale, Crook & Son, Oct.20th 1852* (Extract). Private Collection.

4

1 . 2 -	48	View at Cosham	Shalders	*Copperd* 1.
	49	Study	G. Cole	*1*
1 . 10 . 0	50	Ditto, Landogo on the Wye	G. V. Cole	*D Tucker* 3
	51	Water Color Drawing, " View in Scotland	G. V. Cole	*15/-*
3 . 0 . 0	52	Ditto, " Langdale Pikes, Westmoreland	A. Penley	*Bastable*
	53	Ditto, " Leith Hill, Surrey	G. V. Cole	*15/-* 1
1 . 0 . 0	54	Ditto, New Weir on the Wye"	"	*Randell* 1
1 . 10 -	55	View of Kingley Vale	G. Cole	*1- 10*
	56	A beautiful view of Start Point	G. V. Cole	
	57	Ditto, Babbicombe Bay	"	
	58	View on the Wye at Landogo	"	*1 . 10*
2 . 14 . 0	59	Landscape. Dinner Hour	G. Cole	*M.*
2 . 10 . 0	60	Woking Common	"	*Hall*
3 - 0 - 0	61	Hastings Beach	"	*Turtle*
2 . 0 0	62	Boats and Figures	Shalders	*Hazel*
1 - 10 .	63	Study. View at Southwick	G. Cole	*Turtle*
1 - 10 .	64	View in Goodwood Park	Shalders	*Bastable*
3 . 3 . 0	65	Farriers' Forge by night	G. Cole	*Davis*
2 - 10 .	66	Early Morning. Going to Market	Shalders	*Taylor*
4 . 0 . 0	67	Study of Fruit, after Campadoglio		*Turtle*
. 3 .	68	Study of Fruit	G. Cole	*Smoke*
3 - 10 .	69	View of Portsmouth from Portsdown	G. Cole	*Copperd*
2 . 8 -	70	View near Bramshot	"	*Randall*
3 . 3 .	71	Entrance of Portsmouth Harbour	"	*Hazel*
3 . 3 .	72	View. Welch Scenery	"	*Randall*
1 . 3 .	73	Water Color Drawing, "Southsea Castle, in gilt frame	G. V. Cole	*Smoke*

(which ran a lottery, with the paintings and engravings bought from artists as prizes), to further the sale of his work. In earlier days he had experienced problems with a Dutch merchant who refused to pay for his picture:

> 'The artist said little, but a few days afterwards clapped a pair of wings on the shoulders, and exhibited the picture in a shop-window, with the title "The Flying Dutchman." Crowds of laughing friends testified their appreciation of the portrait and the joke, and the irate subject, accepting the general verdict, was only too glad to have the wings painted out and to pay for his portrait.'

Such setbacks had long been a thing of the past, but encouraged by widening recognition and the hope of greater financial reward, George Cole, his son Vicat, together with George Shalders, sold up and left for the capital in 1852.

CHAPTER 5

'THE CHIEF NAVAL ARSENAL
IN THE WORLD'

40. *The Sketching Class at Portchester*, 1912. University of Portsmouth

The 1870s ushered in a period of unprecedented change to Portsmouth, socially, culturally, and in the appearance of the town itself. Something of the former is captured in a speech made by General Drayson, on the distribution of prizes at the School of Science and Art, 6th February 1890. He began by saying:

> 'He had heard it from a friend that thirty years ago, Portsmouth was stupid and Southsea frivolous.
> That might have been true then, for they had no Free Library, no Literary and Science Society
> [the successor to the Portsmouth and Portsea Literary and Philosophical Society, but
> overwhelmingly scientific in character], and no School of Science and Art, but it could not be said
> of Portsmouth now.'

The School, founded in 1871, as part of a national programme to raise standards in design, was initially based at 5, Pembroke Road, previously known as the Green Row Rooms, next door to the Naval Officers' Club. James Carter, who also taught art at the nearby Grammar School, was its earliest head. The art school moved premises several times before settling as the newly established Portsmouth Municipal School of Art (1895) at the Municipal College behind the Guildhall, in 1908. Much of its

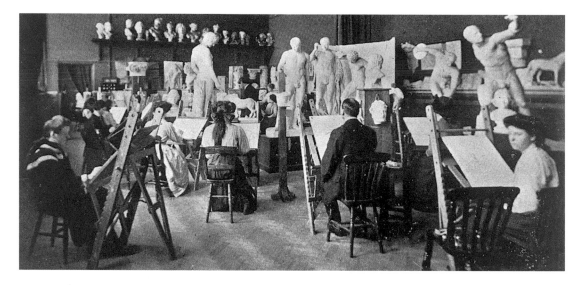

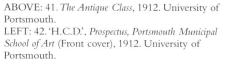

ABOVE: 41. *The Antique Class*, 1912. University of Portsmouth.
LEFT: 42. 'H.C.D.', *Prospectus, Portsmouth Municipal School of Art* (Front cover), 1912. University of Portsmouth.

work was with 14 to 16 year olds, who according to *What to do with the Boy or Girl possessing Artistic Ability* (1917), a leaflet issued by the Council, were destined for apprenticeships in a large range of occupations that included auctioneering, picture dealing, motor body building or in the case of girls as milliners and tracers. Only a minority, aided by scholarships or private means went on to prepare 'for positions as Illustrators, Poster Designers, Scenic Artists or Art Teachers,' and of these even fewer emerged as professional artists. At the same event, the General went on to criticise, 'the flippant manner in which some students went about their work' combined with poor attendance. Perhaps this was due in part to the unimaginative nature of the teaching. Certainly Hubert von Herkomer found much to criticise at the Southampton school where he was sent to study at the age of 14 in 1863, being far from complimentary about the teacher and his approach:

43. *Head Life Class*, 1912. University of Portsmouth.

'He was a tolerably well educated man, but a poor artist; and I think he was the worst judge of art I have ever come across. Under his tuition I was first put to copy those outlines of antique figures, after which I was advanced to drawing from the cast…The teaching in that school was stupid and worthless; and what was particularly bad in my case happened to be the fact that it did not confine itself to the hours when I attended there, as the master gave me his water-colour drawings to take home for copying. Amateurish to the last degree, these drawings were not likely to inspire me. My copies were hastily done, and this often got me into a hopeless muddle.'

His experience compared less favourably to Nina Hamnett's who some years later, spent a term at Portsmouth Municipal School of Art, aged 13, in 1903. She had been taken out of school at Bath to recover from glandular fever, and was with her family at Portsmouth awaiting the return of her father, an army officer, from the Boer War. Nina Hamnett resented the whole approach to teaching, which seemed to reinforce the stuffy conformity of her upbringing and stimulate her own deep seated rebellious instincts, but at least the work of the older students encouraged her to persevere with her own ambitions. Nina was given coloured pictures of Venice to copy in watercolour which soon bored her, so she took to wandering about the Art School where she found a passage on whose walls were hung nude studies by the students, which fired her with enthusiasm. In contrast, the Antique Room with its white plaster casts of Venus, Hercules and the Dancing Faun, filled her with an irresistible desire to get a hammer and chip off the plaster fig leaves that seemed both ugly and silly.

In the 1880s, the painter Edward Burne-Jones, an ardent champion of the Birmingham School of Art, argued that 'A Museum of Art is as essential for a student of art, as a library to the student of letters'. Portsmouth however, had to wait until 1895 until the Town Museum was established in the upper rooms of the old Guildhall in the High Street. The surviving Notebook of Loans (1893–1900), kept by the first Curator, W.H. Saunders, includes works by local painters such as Calcott and Ubsdell,

RIGHT: 44. J.A.M.
Whistler, *Bunting*, 1887.
© Hunterian Museum
and Art Gallery,
University of Glasgow.

BELOW: 45. J.A.M.
Whistler, *Dipping the
Flag*, 1887.
© Hunterian Museum
and Art Gallery,
University of Glasgow.

46. J.A.M. Whistler, *Portsmouth Children*, 1887. © Hunterian Museum and Art Gallery, University of Glasgow.

seascapes by Clarkson Stanfield and E.W. Cooke, the Dutch artists Van de Velde, and Ruysdael, perhaps indicators of gaps in what was still a small collection. Whatever the truth of the matter, the Museum was immensely popular, and had 45,000 visitors a year by 1901. However, the Report of the School of Science and Art (1904) complained that the town still lacked an art gallery and hoped that by the time the new Municipal College opened, this would be rectified and the Council would have decided 'to obtain a small permanent collection of high class works of art and will have inaugurated a periodical loan exhibition where the works of local artists will have a prominent position.'

Frequent reviews of the fleet took place, 18 in all between 1842 and 1914, an average of one every four years. The American artist James McNeill Whistler, as President of the Society of British Artists, attended the Golden Jubilee Review of 1887 in an official capacity, after having successfully petitioned Queen Victoria that June on behalf of the Society, for the prefix 'Royal'. On July 27th he began a series of 12 etchings, mostly drawn from a moving boat, completed on the following day. The sense of atmosphere and lightness of touch in plates such as *Bunting* and *Portsmouth Children* sets them apart from the more conventional work produced for such occasions. The Golden Jubilee, as an onlooker recalled, witnessed:

> 'a wonderful display of ironclads and crafts of all kinds, [and] in the evening after the Royal Yacht had steamed slowly through the long lines of battleships, there was a display of rockets such as, I suppose, was never seen at sea before…The proceedings ended with a fine display of the electric searchlight.'

Whistler himself modestly described his own work as, 'notes as I might say of the needle, not the pen, taken at the moment, and from point to point of that imperial, but pacific, and more than Roman triumph.' A set was presented to the Queen and it is a pity that Edward VII later sold them to settle a gambling debt.

Artists and writers responded in different ways to the changes of these decades. Henry James, after a few hours spent in the vicinity of the Dockyard c.1879, wrote:

> 'I was distressed to perceive that a famous seaport could be at once untidy and prosaic. Portsmouth is dirty but it is also dull…The dockyard, into which I was unable to penetrate, is a colossal enclosure, signalised externally by a grim brick wall, as featureless as an empty blackboard. The dockyard eats up the town, as it were, and there is nothing left over but the gin shops, which the town drinks up. There is not even a crooked old quay of any consequence, with brightly-patched houses looking out upon a forest of masts…I had another hour or so before my train departed, and it would have gone hard with me if I had not bethought myself of hiring a boat and being pulled about in the harbour. Here a certain amount of entertainment was to be found. There were great ironclads and white troopships that looked vague and spectral, like the floating home of the Flying Dutchman, and small, devilish vessels whose mission was to project the infernal torpedo.'

Finally James went on board the *Victory*, but even this experience proved less than satisfactory: 'Bank Holiday is now her great date; once upon a time it was Trafalgar…Now, it was hardly more than a mere source of income to Portsmouth watermen, an objective point for Whitsuntide excursionists, a thing a pilgrim from afar must allude to very casually, for fear of seeming vulgar or even quite serious.'

However, the more prosaic *Where Shall We Go, A Guide To The Watering Places of England* (1892) whilst warning the visitor against the negative aspects of the town, 'barracks, prisons, unions, railways and the like', enthused over Southsea:

> 'It would not be rustic or romantic enough for all tastes, but recommends itself to many by the stir of military and naval life which is its salient feature. What with regimental bands, parades, and reviews by land, and the Solent continually alive with yachts, steamboats, and ships of war, it can never be dull…' [praising the Common], 'which with its pier at each end, its artifical lake [the Canoe Lake], and its esplanade along the shore, has such a cheerful outlook on the Solent and the Isle of Wight,' [and describing the harbour] as 'a place of pilgrimage, with Nelson's *Victory* for a shrine.'

Paintings such as Eyre Crowe's *Convicts at Work, Portsmouth* (1887), and Herkomer in his preliminary study for *Missing* (1880), showing weeping families outside the Dockyard awaiting news of the loss of the training ship *Atlanta,* provide glimpses of the harsher sides of life at this period, that had only a limited appeal to the picture buying public, who preferred less uncomfortable themes. Likewise the moral ambiguities in works by Tissot such as *The Ball on Shipboard* (c.1874), set during Cowes Week, where the artist believed the most fashionable society in England was to be found, and *The Gallery of HMS Calcutta (Portsmouth)* (1876), raised questions of behaviour that made critics uneasy. Of the former picture, one wrote: 'The girls who are spread about in every attitude are evidently the "high life below stairs of the port," – who have borrowed their mistresses dresses for the nonce', and another complained that some were revealing an unseemly amount of flesh for daylight hours. Many wondered if the underlying subject of *The Gallery* was some sort of intrigue, and to the same extent this was the case with *How Happy I could be with Either* (1877), originally an etching, the painted version of which, *Portsmouth Dockyard* (c.1877), shows a cheerful looking Highland sergeant of the

47. Eyre Crowe,
Convicts at Work,
Portsmouth, 1887.
By courtesy of the
Trafalgar Galleries.

Black Watch Regiment rowing two female companions across the harbour, turning to the woman of his choice, to her companion's vexation [Plate 18]. *HMS Calcutta,* recently made an experimental gunnery ship, is visible in the background. Ruskin condemned Tissot's conversation pieces as 'mere coloured photographs of vulgar society', while Eyre Crowe and Herkomer's social realism, made their middle class audience equally uncomfortable. In Portsmouth as elsewhere, less controversial themes were likely to provide an artist with a livelihood. The sketchbooks of one such painter, Harry Coish, are a visual chronicle of everyday life in the 1880s and although his works such as *Portsmouth Harbour* (1881) are within the accepted conventions of marine painting, his drawings reveal a very different side to his

48. Hubert von Herkomer, *Missing*, c.1880. By courtesy of the Witt Library, (H.J. Cornish collection), Courtauld Institute, London.

RIGHT: 49. James Tissot, *The Gallery of H.M.S 'Calcutta' (Portsmouth)*, 1876. Tate ©, London 2008.
BELOW: 50. Harry Coish, *May Day Celebrations at Portsmouth, the procession passing through Fratton. Firemen leading followed by the Corporation horses*, n.d .Portsmouth City Museums.

character, a limitless curiosity that allowed him to cram his sketchbooks with events ranging from the May Day Celebrations passing through Fratton, the *Forth* Court Martial (portrait sketches of the main protagonists), the recovery of the drowned body of John Wenn, and the Portsea Building Society crash. Delicate pencil drawings of old buildings, and the demolition of the *Bellerophon*, are followed by episodes such as the burial of privates William Davies and James Rogers, who had been overwhelmed by a snowstorm, ships' figureheads, the newly opened People's Park (Victoria Park), and the Watch House at Russell's Oyster Beds, Langstone, to mention but a few examples taken from a single volume.

In contrast, his contemporary William Edward Atkins, who like Coish was born in the town, provided a more predictable chronology of these years in a series of ship paintings at a time of

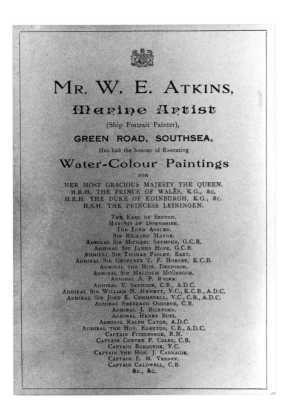

ABOVE: 51. *Business Card for W.E. Atkins,* n.d. Portsmouth City Records Office.
BELOW: 52. W.E. Atkins, *The Reserve Squadron Reviewed by Queen Victoria,* 1878. Portsmouth City Museums.

rising imperialism. Atkins included members of the Royal family and numerous high ranking naval officers among his patrons. It would be strange if he had not been encouraged to paint the Diamond Jubilee Review of 1897, particularly since the celebrations were on such a spectacular scale, with even more ships taking part than in the Golden Jubilee ten years previously. A contemporary, James Yates, records:

> '…an immense assemblage of warships…which stretched in four lines from Spithead to Cowes. Numbers of passenger ships brought visitors, but anchored in the vicinity. There was a constant stream of sightseeing vessels passing up and down the lines, and it was a grand sight when all was cleared, to see the Royal procession of yachts and attendant steamers pass along the centre of the lines, all the ships being fully dressed with flags and outlined by rows of standing men on the decks, bridges and yards. In the evening the whole fleet was illuminated.'

The Reserve Squadron Reviewed by Queen Victoria (1878), like *Indian Troopship* (1884), represents Atkins's more formal style, unlike *Panoramic View from the Black Horse Tavern to Victoria Pier* and *Hay Barge* which are perhaps more appealing to present

53. *Tower House*, 1919. Private Collection.

day taste [Plates 19 and 20]. Unfortunately, the artist ran into financial difficulties in the late 1880s, possibly as a result of the growing popularity of photography, but continued to paint at least until 1905. Competition with photography does not seem to have hindered the career of another contemporary, William Lionel Wyllie, who settled in Portsmouth in 1906, remaining there until his death in 1931.

Wyllie's reputation was already well established when he bought Tower House near the Point in 1906. He had first been to Portsmouth in 1871, and it is clear from the letter he wrote to his father, and the comments of his future wife, Marion, that he was fascinated by the hulks and other decaying ships in the upper end of the harbour [Plate 21]:

> 'I have been doing three pictures, but it seems to me they "want subjects" [here he makes three very neat little pen-and-ink sketches of the picture, the first of Southsea Casle, with a big flag flying on a flagstaff, and the lighthouse alongside on a slight eminence, and rough hillocks of common all round. The second little sketch is a view of the harbour overlooking the Solent, with the old men-o'-war in a group drying their sails; the third looking along Hamilton Bank with Gilkicker fort in the distance.]' Bill goes on, 'I must stick in a lot of boats and things. We went up the harbour today in a boat, and saw all the ships and hulks, King George's old yacht, and the Queen's yacht and the Prince of Wales's fishing-boat, such a swell! Then we came home to roast leg of mutton and apple pie.'

[Then Marion adds,] 'The great interest in the letter is that on the blank half-sheets he has Made Delicate pen-and-ink sketches of some of the men-o'-war, now long since broken up; the *Minotaur* with five masts, the first three with sails drying on the yard-arms, and the two masts aft flying signals. Below *Minotaur* comes *Victory*, and below again some of the ships in Rotten Row that used to be alongside each other, painted a uniform yellow ochre with brilliant green bottoms. To these he adds a sketch of the Prince of Wales's fishing-boat, and the old *Royal Sovereign* with her great width and three funny round turrets, two derricks and one funnel, forming part of the naval history of over sixty years ago.'

The results of this trip were two paintings *Rotten Row* and *The Old Bellerophen* that were accepted by the Royal Academy when Wyllie was just 19½ years old.

Wyllie returned to this theme many times, most notably in a more ambitious oil (1880), but he was not only interested in past naval glories, but in modern craft large and small. His many talents were recognised when he succeeded W.E. Atkins as Portsmouth's Marine Artist and Shipping Correspondent for the *Graphic*. Moreover he was not a mere painter of ships, his ability to catch the atmosphere of water and sky in a conscious attempt to emulate Turner, putting him in another category altogether [Plate 22]. His experience in sailing and building boats also proved invaluable to him, according to Peter Anson, a fellow artist working in Portsmouth:

'W.L Wyllie, R.A., the famous marine artist was still living at Tower House at the entrance to the harbour, where the water lapped against the terrace, and from whose windows there was a fascinating view over Spithead. He was in his seventy-seventh year, but still active and vigorous. It was no uncommon sight to see this venerable old man, with his bronzed face and white beard, going off for a sail with his troop of Sea Scouts. He never seemed to mind my watching him while he was painting or making etching. It was an inspiration to stand beside him and study his methods. That year [1927] he was finishing his big painting of the British fleet off Jutland, and was turning out many watercolours and etchings made at sea; all of them so alive and breezy.'

54. *W.L. Wyllie Working in his Studio, Tower House, c.*1928. Private Collection.

The original Dreadnought was launched at Portsmouth in 1909, and five of its successors, including *HMS Bellerophen in Portsmouth Harbour with Victory in the background*, were painted by Wyllie in his most monumental style. No further capital ships left the Yard after 1915 and for the remainder of the First World War it reverted to its role of repair and refitting, with the exception of the building of submarines. The workforce mushroomed from 10,000 in 1911 to 23,000 by 1918 and it was into this vast complex of ships, men and machines, that a very different artist, John D. Fergusson, one of a small group later known as the Scottish Colourists, now ventured.

Fergusson was never an official war artist, but was given permission by the authorities to come down to Portsmouth and paint a series of battleships and submarines, as part of a campaign to boost the war effort. He arrived on 30th July 1918, and left on August 20th, staying at the George in the High Street. The weather was fine, and Southsea particularly to his taste, its villas reminding him of those happy times he had spent in the south of France. He was greatly impressed by what he saw in the Dockyard, and quickly fixed on several subjects to paint, though much to his annoyance he was frequently hindered by over zealous workmen reporting him to the police for spying (for as yet his naval officer's uniform had not arrived).

On the 1st of August, in a letter to Margaret Morris, his future wife, he wrote, '…everything is going well with me. I went round and saw everything and fixed on several splendid things – one in particular – and it's arranged that I start work at once, so my anxiety is over.' By 6th August he had seen enough to tell Alfred Yockney at the Ministry of Information, 'I'm going to give you plenty of interesting work and stuff that has not been done <u>at all.</u> You can count on it being perfectly <u>reasonable</u> <u>even</u> exact. I don't think there's any other way to do the stuff.' The surviving pictures show clearly what captured Fergusson's imagination, often in colours that stem directly from his association with the Fauves in pre-war Paris, together with a fascination with the machinery of war to which he gives a dominant, often menacing quality that owes something to the Futurists, giving his work a contemporary, exciting feel. *Portsmouth Docks, 1918* is dominated by a huge crane, and the prow of a destroyer that completely dwarf a small group of people gathered on the quayside below. *A Damaged Destroyer* uses the same formula to good effect. In contrast *Blue Submarine, Portsmouth* has a Mediterranean feel about it, in its use of colour, the sailors in their white uniforms, the vessel itself a bright blue. The middle ground with its sailing boats, orange and white, a reminder of more peaceful times, yet more warships in the background, and a barrage balloon floating in the clouds above, quickly remind us of the actual context. Its companion *Three Submarines* is far more menacing, their shark like quality emphasized by the artist's use of black and white.

In the 1920s Wyllie played an important part in establishing the Society for Nautical Research, and as an early committee member took an active part in the campaign for the preservation of *HMS Victory* in dry dock at Portsmouth, making two etchings of the ship to help raise the necessary funds, as well as a poster showing the *Renown* and the *Victory* for the Southern Railway Company and the City Council in 1928 [Plates 23 and 24]. But perhaps his proudest achievement was the *Trafalgar* diorama, that can be seen in the Royal Naval Museum. The Portsmouth and Hampshire Art Society was founded in 1909 under his guidance. Wyllie was its first President and by 1935, four years after his death, membership amounted to about 110. By then the Council had acquired Cumberland House (1928), the upper floor of which was used for exhibitions, while the Museum had benefited from the Bashford Bequest, a small extension added to the building that became known as the Bashford Gallery, that as well as housing a collection of family portraits also held paintings from the

55. J.D. Fergusson,
Portsmouth Docks,
1918. University
of Stirling.
Courtesy of The
Fergusson Gallery,
Perth & Kinross
Council.

permanent collection. In the 1930s the Museum contained examples of marine, landscape painting and portraiture, but few 20th century works by local or other artists, yet these developments taken together all helped promote the cause of art in the town more effectively.

From the 1860s Southsea continued to expand its amenities, attracting more visitors in the process. Clarence Pier was built in 1861 on the site of King's Rooms, followed by South Parade Pier in 1876, and in the 1880s the Ladies Mile and the Canoe Lake were created. 'The Gem of England's Watering Places' owed at least some of its popularity to the artists who provided illustrations for a series of guidebooks, and other publications as well as individual engravings published by Charpentier for over

The old Garrison Bakery in King St., now known as "Peter Rice's" Yard.

ABOVE: 56. Martin Snape, *Globe Yard, Oyster Street*, n.d. Portsmouth City Museums.

RIGHT: 57. Alick Summers, *The Guildhall from Commercial Road*, 1936. Portsmouth City Museums.

OPPOSITE PAGE: 58. Peter Anson, *The Camber, Portsmouth*, 1929. The Moray Council Museums Service.

a hundred years – including works by James Calcott, William Mitchell, and later, Martin Snape. Few of Calcott's other works survive, not so Snape whose watercolours and drawings have been praised for their vividness and honesty, an impressive record of both Gosport and Portsmouth, not only of historic buildings, but also of a landscape much of which has disappeared. One of Wyllie's final works, *The Old Portsmouth and The New Southsea*, was given away with copies of the Council's 1932 Southsea guide, perhaps in part a celebration of the town's recently acquired city status in 1926. He provided both text and paintings, donating the originals to the City 'to form part of a permanent Wyllie exhibit in the Portsmouth Art Gallery.' Subjects included were the harbour, main gate of the Dockyard, the Camber, and of course the *Victory*. In all they are a skilful blend of the old and the new, although Southsea is represented solely by an aerial view of the Canoe Lake with South Parade Pier in the background, all in a traditional illustrative style. Not so Alick Summers's *Point, Portsmouth*, very characteristic of the poster art of the period in its paring down of subject matter and strong emphasis on solid colours, painted for the *NUT Conference Guide* (1937), as the event was held in the town [Plates 25 and 26].

To varying degrees the work of Wyllie, Anson, Snape and Summers reflects some of the many changes influencing painting since the 1870s, a gradual blurring of the lines between 'artistic' and

LEFT: 59. Martin Snape, *The Camber Dock and Electricity Generating Station*, 1894. Portsmouth City Museums.
BELOW LEFT: 60. George Horne, *Palmerston Road*, c.1932. Portsmouth City Museums.

commercial subject matter. More generally there was a breakdown of boundaries, and a revolt against academic conventions often involving challenging techniques and styles, beginning with the Impressionists and asserting the primacy of everyday life as legitimate subject matter, or 'the ugly and the vulgar' as their opponents called it. D.T. Rose's watercolour *St. Thomas's Cathedral*, shows men clearing away rubble from bomb damage in the High Street while a later study of the Floating Bridge focuses on the two men adjusting the mighty chains on which safety depended, a subject also explored by Garrick Palmer in *Portsmouth-Gosport Floating Bridge* (1962). H.E. Young's studies of shipping at the Camber in the 1920s, emphasize the workmen and sailors engaged in their tasks, and Martin Snape's watercolour of the same dock shows the newly constructed Central Electricity Station in the background. George Horne's etching *Palmerston Road* (1932), bustles with shoppers going about their business, as does Alick Summers's *The Guildhall from Commercial Road* (1936). Neither Edward King nor Violet Pearse shrank from revealing the destruction caused by enemy bombing during the Second World War. Thus, relying on the evidence of art alone, more is known about the appearance of Portsmouth and the lives of its inhabitants from the 1870s onwards than at any previous period in its history.

CHAPTER 6

THE SECOND WORLD WAR
AND AFTER

Between 1940 and 1942 Portsmouth lost 6,500 properties to enemy bombing, among which were six churches, the three main shopping centres, the City Museum in the High Street with most of its collections, while many other buildings including the Guildhall were badly damaged. Yet in 1941 at the height of the blitz, Admiral Sir William James, Naval Commander in Chief at Portsmouth, successfully organised an art exhibition of work by Royal Naval personnel and Dockyardmen, which he opened on 8th August. Some 400 works mainly oils, watercolours and posters were submitted, the standard of work was high and a number were sold, a poignant testimony to the public interest in art, even in wartime. By 1944, when the last raid took place, Portsmouth was reckoned to be the eighth most blitzed city in Britain. Further demolition and rebuilding took place in the immediate postwar years to be followed by economic and other changes in the 1970s and '80s that were to change the city beyond recognition.

Some of the hectic atmosphere that characterised the early months of the war emerges from the letters of Eric Ravilious, made an official war artist with the rank of captain in the Royal Navy and sent to *HMS Dolphin* in summer 1940 – a coincidence, since his former tutor at the Royal College, Paul Nash, also an official war artist, had been posted to Gosport as a captain in the Hampshire Regiment in 1916 (and later invalided home from France to a spell at the Queen Alexandra Hospital) [Plate 27]. At first Ravilious seems to have been somewhat daunted, or as he put it, 'I've just arrived at this place which is almost overwhelming in size and variety. I feel like an earwig setting out to draw Buckingham Palace.' However, within a few days his mood had changed and he confided to his wife Tirzah on 23rd July:

> 'The weather is marvellous and I am torn between both interiors and landscapes, I mean seascapes, and make rather a mess of both. Interiors are not easy. You must get them dark enough, and I feel I've drawn enough at sea. The variety here is overwhelming. I wish someone would give me orders sometimes about painting to lessen the responsibility. I'm trying too many sorts of things probably. The air raids are no help and we have to run for it to shelter and that is a great bore at night as lights all go out in three minutes. I've no torch so strike matches. Today as the siren blew I ran into Augustus Courtauld [the Arctic explorer and a wartime lieutenant in the RNVR] and shall be dining in his mess this evening.
>
> They are taking me out in an MTB tomorrow. They go like the wind and wet you to the skin. God send I'm not sick as well.'

Within a matter of days Ravilious decided to concentrate on submarine interiors, and hoped to

61. Edward King, *Hampshire and Jubilee Terraces*, 1941/3. Portsmouth City Museums.

have some sketches for his wife, when she came to stay. In general when he had local leave they put up at the George (now no more), or the Keppel's Head on the Hard, and whether at work or otherwise his enjoyment of life comes through in surviving correspondence. Early in August his work was making steady progress, as he told his friend Helen Binyon:

> 'The submarine has taken such a lot of doing, but now there are half a dozen drawings on the way, of interiors (with people!) whether good or not I don't know. I rather enjoy the sea trips though it gets awfully hot and noisy and a very peculiar submarine smell when she dives. There is hardly room to move of course, so drawings have to be hasty. There is something jolly good about them if only I can manage it: a blue gloom with coloured lights and everyone in shirts and braces. People go to sleep in odd positions across tables.'

By 6th August Ravilious had six or seven sketches completed to his satisfaction, but had come to the conclusion that 'submarine drawing is uphill work' and was looking for fresh challenges. The resulting collection that possibly included previous work, was published in the following year as a children's book. It is a pity that he did not have time to paint in the countryside, or even the coastal fortifications as he did at Newhaven and Dover, where he was far more effective in displaying his talents.

In 1941 Lady Margaret Daly, the Lady Mayoress, and Dr Beaton, Head of St James's Hospital, invited one of its inmates, the artist Edward King, to put on record the damage inflicted on the city in a series of paintings, some 40 of which remain in Portsmouth Museum. King already had a distinguished career behind him when he was committed to the asylum in 1925/6 at the age of 64. In earlier, happier days he had joined the New English Art Club whose members included Sickert, Augustus John and Wilson Steer, and later the Plein Air movement at St Ives in Cornwall. Both groups were deeply influenced by the Impressionists in their style and subject matter, and he had exhibited

TOP LEFT: 62. Edward King, *Ruins of St Thomas's Street*, 1941/3. Portsmouth City Museums.
BOTTOM LEFT: 63. Edward King, *Guildhall from Russell Street*, 1941/3. Portsmouth City Museums.
ABOVE: 64. Edward King, *Houseboats at Milton alongside a Quay with a Girl in Red*, 1946. Portsmouth City Museums.

and sold many pictures. King, always accompanied by an attendant followed the trail of destruction, painting a series of dramatic works in which hot ochres and flaming reds are the dominant colours, with titles that are deceptively prosaic, *Hampshire and Jubilee Terraces*, *Ruins of St Thomas's Street*, to give but two instances. Later he was allowed to paint in St James's grounds and the neighbourhood, now unaccompanied, where he produced more varied work including landscapes of the hospital farm and houseboats in Langstone Harbour, that hark back in spirit to his earlier life [Plates 28 and 29].

If King's work owed much of its impact to the use of colour, that of Violet Pearse formed a complete contrast, black and white etchings with an economy of line that bring out the harsh results of the destruction of Portsmouth's main shopping centres just as effectively, particularly in her etchings of Commercial Road and King's Road at the height of the blitz in 1943, the absence of people in both adding to the sense of desolation.

Not all artists responded to the war in this way: Eric Rimmington's mural of an imaginary scene at Portsmouth Railway Station in 1949, painted at the former Trafalgar Services Club in Edinburgh Road, has been highly praised for its unrivalled ability to capture 'the essence of Portsmouth' in this decade. In a composition that owes a debt to Stanley Spencer's work at the Sandham Memorial Chapel, Burghclere, Rimmington has grouped a number of sailors, soldiers and civilians against a background depicting the history of the city, that feature Southsea Castle in 1545, the High Street in

ABOVE: 65. Violet Pearse, *Commercial Road, Portsmouth*, 1943. Portsmouth City Museums.
TOP RIGHT: 66. W.A. Jefferies, *The Construction of a Floating Dock, H.M Dockyard, Portsmouth*, 1966. Portsmouth City Museums.
BOTTOM RIGHT: 67. W.A. Jefferies, *Navigation Light*, c.1963. Portsmouth City Museums.

the eighteenth century, and the Guildhall and rooftops of Portsmouth in 1939. It is the anecdotal character of the work that is its chief appeal, its homage to ordinary people of that era going about their everyday lives, and some have seen particular symbolism in the child climbing the staircase as perhaps an optimistic portent of the town's future [Plate 30].

But what sort of future? For the rebirth of the city in the '50s and '60s not only resulted in an extensive building programme, but was accompanied by other changes, both economic and social. Among the results were the disappearance of the Floating Bridge and older ferries to the Isle of Wight. However they live on in the paintings of W.A. Jefferies, whose enthusiasm for shipping is a common factor in paintings as varied as *Car Ferry to the Isle of Wight* (c. 1959) [Plate 31], *B.R. Jetty, Portsmouth* (c.1960), *The Construction of a Floating Dock, H.M. Dockyard, Portsmouth* (1966) and *Navigation Light* (c.1963), his fascination with their workings, that also recalls his early architectural training. The new car ferries and hovercraft belong to a different age, likewise the Dockyard, which since the Defence Review of 1981 has a drastically reduced workforce, while from 1985 onwards the historic areas of the yard have been run by the Portsmouth Naval Base Property Trust. So these examples of John Green's paintings, based on his own experiences working there, *Yard Boy Rigger* (2003), and *Cruiser in No.15 Dock* (2002) recall a world recognisable to the Victorians and just as remote to us in many respects [Plate 32]. Portsmouth has changed in other ways, the area around the Camber is partly residential, altered beyond recognition from the busy scene displayed in earlier paintings, and the Gunwharf is now given over to housing, shopping, and other forms of

68. John Green, *Yard Boy Rigger*, 2003.
© John Green.

entertainment. The Solent Garrison ceased to exist in 1961 and the military had disappeared from the city by the end of the decade. The gradual decline of the traditional seaside holiday has led to an increasing reliance on heritage tourism, and the largest single employer is now the University, heir to educational developments going back to the 1870s.

In the past, artistic activity in Portsmouth was limited by the absence of a large middle class, the result of the town's dependence on the Dockyard, a government establishment not run for profit, and whose policy of self sufficiency further curtailed opportunities for money making by contractors. No bodies comparable to the Plymouth Institution or Liverpool Academy were established to encourage public patronage through regular exhibitions or the awarding of prizes, often later becoming the nuclei of municipal art galleries and museums. The Victorian Corporation had never aspired to be patrons of art. A portrait of the Queen by George Swandale was accepted by the Council in 1838, and hung in the new Town Hall, but the money was to be raised by public subscription. Two years later, Sir George Staunton, an M.P. for the town, presented the Corporation with his portrait, by the same artist. In 1844 Schetky, during the visit of Louis Philippe, attempted to interest the authorities in a painting for the Town Hall, but apparently the project came to nothing. The bulk of the pictures later acquired were portraits, often gifts by members of parliament, or of local celebrities such as Sir Walter Besant and Charles Dickens, former mayors and various national figures such as Agnes Weston and Lord Roberts.

Portsmouth had to wait almost until the end of the nineteenth century for a museum, while the upper floor of Cumberland House was hardly a substitute for a municipal art gallery, although, (following its re-opening in 1952), it continued to host exhibitions of work by local and other artists. During the 1960s there were various plans to include a municipal museum and art gallery

69. *Portsmouth College of Art*, 1960.
University of Portsmouth

in the redevelopment of the Guildhall Square, but these came to nothing, and it was decided to take over part of the former Clarence Barracks in what is now Pembroke Park. The building was successfully adapted, and opened to the public in 1972. Fortunately the Municipal School of Art (later Portsmouth College of Art and from 1966, Portsmouth College of Art and Design), made far steadier progress, numbers rising from c.150 full and part-time students in 1900 to c.1000 in 1960. This expansion together with increasing public funding, resulted in the impressive new building in Hyde Park Road which was opened by Sir Kenneth (later Lord) Clark, 2nd November 1960.

The growth of art education in the last century, coincided with the establishment of the Portsmouth and Hampshire Art Society. Wyllie was succeeded as President by his daughter, Aileen, and today his grandson John is one of the Vice Presidents. Today its membership is well over 200 and it still provides opportunities for members (professional and amateur alike) to exhibit, take part in regular classes and workshops, and visit exhibitions in London and elsewhere. Among its more notable members were George Henry Downing, its first Secretary, W.A. Jefferies, Violet Pearse and William Grant. Downing was a pupil at the School of Art in 1904, and taught art at the Southern Secondary School for Boys from 1915 onwards. Eric Rimmington was one of his pupils and later studied at the Southern College of Art (as the Portsmouth College was then known). Wilfred Jefferies had a more varied career, training in London and Paris, Head of Drawing at the Art College for much of the 1930s, and later art master at the same school from 1945 until his retirement. William Grant was a pupil at the School of Art in 1912 and later a Vice President of the Portsmouth and Hampshire Art Society, while Violet Pearse, also a member of the Society is said to have taught art at Portsmouth Grammar School, some of her work surviving in the school's archive. Alick Summers was Treasurer of the Society in 1935;

70. *The Library,*
Portsmouth College of
Art, 1960. University
of Portsmouth.

Garrick Palmer studied at the College in the 1950s and a fellow student, William Fulljames, has left some recollections of those years. (See Appendix 4, below). Private galleries, sustained by this widening interest in art, continued to hold exhibitions. The Southsea born artist Peter Anson held an exhibition of paintings and drawings of marine subjects at a local gallery in the autumn of 1927 (See Appendix 3, below). Clearly this met with success as he became a regular contributor to many London and provincial exhibitions thereafter, eventually being elected a founder member of the Society of Marine Artists. Anson was but one of many painters, who now had advantages in terms of training and opportunities to exhibit unknown to their predecessors, while continuing to enjoy what Portsmouth and its neighbourhood had to offer.

TOP: Plate 1. George Chambers, *Entrance to Portsmouth Harbour*, 1835. Portsmouth City Museums.
ABOVE: Plate 2. William Daniell, *View from Portsdown Hill*, 1823. Portsmouth City Museums.

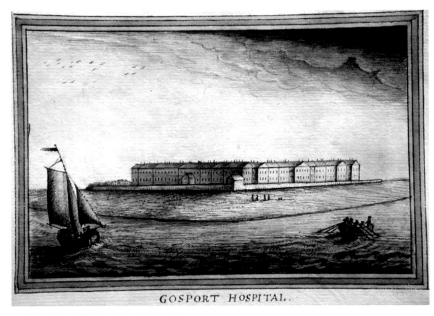

GOSPORT HOSPITAL.

ABOVE: Plate 5. Anon, *Town Hall from the North East*, 1830. Portsmouth City Museums.

LEFT: Plate 6. John Swete, *Gosport Hospital*, 'from the Great Cabbin of the 'Royal George', 1777. Courtesy of the Royal Institution of Cornwall, Courtney Library.

TOP LEFT: Plate 3. William Grant, *Langstone Mill*, n.d. Private Collection.
LEFT: Plate 4. John Clevely Junr., *View of His Majesty's Dockyard at Portsmouth*, n.d. Portsmouth City Museums.

TOP: Plate 7. Louis Garneray, *Prison Hulks in Portsmouth Harbour*, c.1810. Portsmouth City Museums.
ABOVE: Plate 8. R.H.C. Ubsdell, *July 22 1847 Abolition of Free Mart Fair*. Portsmouth City Museums.

TOP: Plate 9. Thomas Rowlandson, *Portsmouth Point*, c.1800. Portsmouth City Museums.

ABOVE: Plate 10. Richard Livesay, *Military Review of the Worcestershire Regiment by Major-General Whitelock, 14 October 1800, on Southsea Common*. Portsmouth City Museums.

TOP: Plate 11. J.C. Schetky, *Portsmouth Harbour*, 1822 Portsmouth City Museums.
ABOVE: Plate 12. J.M.W. Turner, *The Disembarkation of Louis-Philippe at Portsmouth*, c.1844–45. Tate London © 2008.
TOP RIGHT: Plate 13. W. Clarkson Stanfield, *Entrance to Portsmouth Harbour*, 1829. Portsmouth City Museums.
RIGHT: Plate 14. George Cole, *The London Road, Portsdown Hill*, 1867. Portsmouth City Museums.

TOP. Plate 15. R.H.C. Ubsdell, *Volunteer Review*, 1868. Portsmouth City Museums.

ABOVE: Plate 16. Richard Poate, *Dr W.C. Engledue, chairman at the banquet held in 9.1856 to welcome home other ranks from the Crimea, proposing the Royal Toast*. Portsmouth City Museums.

TOP RIGHT: Plate 17. William Smyth, *On the Point, Portsmouth*, 1857. Portsmouth City Museums.

RIGHT: Plate 18. James Tissot, *Portsmouth Dockyard*, c.1877. Tate London © 2008.

ABOVE: Plate 19.
W.E. Atkins, *Panoramic View from the Black Horse Tavern to Victoria Pier*, 1884. Portsmouth City Museums.

RIGHT: Plate 20.
W.E. Atkins, *Hay Barge*, n.d. Portsmouth City Museums.

ABOVE: Plate 21. W.L. Wyllie, *Old Hulks, Portsmouth*, 1880. Portsmouth City Museums.

LEFT: Plate 22. J.D. Fergusson, *Blue Submarine, Portsmouth*, 1918. Courtesy of the Fergusson Gallery, Perth & Kinross Council.

OPPOSITE PAGE TOP: Plate 23.
W.L. Wyllie, *Spit Fort*, 1931. Portsmouth City
Museums.

OPPOSITE PAGE BOTTOM: Plate 24.
W.L. Wyllie, *H.M.S. 'Victory' and
H.M.S. 'Renown'*, 1928. Portsmouth City
Museums.

ABOVE: Plate 25. W. Marston Derrick,
Clarence Pier, 1897. Portsmouth City
Museums.

LEFT: Plate 26. Alick Summers, *Point,
Portsmouth*, 1936. Portsmouth City Museums.

ABOVE TOP: Plate 27. Eric Ravilious, *The Ward Room (2)*, 1940. Collections Imperial War Museum © DACS.
ABOVE: Plate 28. Edward King, *The Connaught Drill Hall, Stanhope Road*, 1941/3. Portsmouth City Museums.

ABOVE TOP: Plate 29. Edward King, *The Grounds of St James's Hospital*, n.d. Portsmouth City Museums.
ABOVE: Plate 30. Eric Rimmington, *Trafalgar House Mural*, 1949 (Detail). Photograph by Alex Saunderson.

TOP: Plate 31. W.A. Jefferies, *Car Ferry to the Isle of Wight*, c.1959. Portsmouth City Museums.
ABOVE: Plate 32. John Green, *Cruiser in No.16 Dock*, 2002. © John Green.

APPENDIX 1

James Northcote and his sitters, May to September 1776, taken from the artist's sitters book, printed in Stephen Gwynn's *Memorials of an Eighteenth Century Painter James Northcote*, (1898), pp.265–266.

Name	Occupation/or that of husband/or relative
1. John Hunt and Antony Hunt (in one picture)	Dockyard official
2. Edward Hunt	Ditto
3. Miss Fitzherbert	M.P. and contractor
4. Miss Jane Fitzherbert	Ditto
5. Mr Fitzherbert	Ditto
6. Master Eyres	Attorney(?)
7. Miss Eyres	Ditto
8. Miss Prosser and Miss L. Prosser (in one picture)	Attorney
9. Mrs Prosser	Ditto
10. Master Josh. Hunt	Dockyard official
11. Mrs Hunt	Ditto
12. Mr Parlby	Contractor
13. Ditto	Ditto
14. Mrs Parlby	Ditto
15. Mr W. Templar	Contractor
16. Ditto	Contractor
17. James Ferguson (the print by Hayward)	Philosopher
18. Miss Moore	Victualler(?)
19. Lord Holmes	Politician
20. Lady Holmes	Ditto
21. Lady Christian (small)	Naval officer
22. Captain Inglefield	Merchantman(?)
23. Captain C. Hamilton	Army officer
24. Ditto	Ditto
25. Captain Chic. Fortescue	Naval officer
26. Captain Piere Williams	Ditto
27. Miss Williams	Ditto
28. Mr Hawker	'Organist at Portsmouth'
29. Rev. Mr Ramsay	Cleric

APPENDIX 2

Gilpin and his contemporaries would have recognised both the route taken and the pre-occupations of Henry Dawson and his younger son Alfred on this mid-Victorian painting tour.

'In September, 1856, he [Henry Dawson] took the writer out again, starting on the 10th for a most delightful walking tour up the Thames. We stayed at Reading a night, then took the railway to Winchester, which though much admired, gave no fresh subjects; then Southampton, where we stayed three days, sketching Netley Abbey, which was then in a wild, natural state: then we walked to Portsmouth, and very weary was the writer at the end of it. A pair of brigs were tacking so prettily against a south wind right down Southampton Water, putting about a dozen times or more, their sails taking as many positions in the sun. The steam-tugs have spoilt all that. Then we jumped into a little boat on Gosport Hard, and sailed across into a vast crowd of similar boats on the Portsmouth Hard. How very lively and moving was the old style, when there were no iron-clads, and the horrid railway station and siding on its row of iron sticks did not go right across the view. Going over the Dockyard, Dawson met a very old friend, John Plowright, a member of the Nottingham Choral Society. He was overlooking the machinery, but he got no great encouragement, as the favoured ones got all the pay and credit, while he had the work and the bumps. At Portsmouth we were rowed up the harbour round the *St Vincent* man-o'-war, but he had already got a sketch when there with his eldest son, Henry, in 1854. One morning on the Southsea beach we saw the *Warrior* go out, grandly smothering herself with smoke. It was very rough at the time, and this was the last episode in the Crimean War. One evening, not long after, Dawson made a fine Indian-ink drawing of this *Warrior* going out. She was one of the first ironclads, and we saw, under Plowright's guidance, the further steps in that direction in the shape of the floating batteries so called. We returned about September 23rd.'

Alfred Dawson, *The Life of Henry Dawson Landscape Painter 1811–1878* (1891), pp.71–72.

APPENDIX 3

Peter Anson was born at Southsea 22nd August 1889, the eldest son of Admiral Charles Anson and Evelyn Ross, and following early training as an architect, he joined the Anglican Benedictine community on Caldey Island, off the coast of Pembrokeshire, becoming a Roman Catholic in 1913, and co-founding the Apostleship of the Sea in 1921. From 1924 onwards he became more involved with drawing shipping of all kinds. At this time he was living mostly in Scotland, but returned briefly to Portsmouth in 1927. He was a great admirer of Wyllie though his approach to art was very different, most obviously in its precision, his water colours in subtle pastels, often scaled down from photographs he had previously taken. A major part of his life was taken up with recording the lives of fishermen and their communities in Ireland after World War I, and Scotland, where he spent the last five years of his life attempting to finish a 'Panorama' of the industry, developing a realistic style aimed at making his work accessible to the widest possible public.

In July 1927 he moved into Anson House in the High Street, and between then and November was busy preparing for an exhibition. The painter's diary though little more than a memorandum book gives a good idea of how he spent his time. Between 22nd and 29th July he was busy sketching onion boats and a collier at the Camber, before making a brief working visit to Gosport. In August Anson worked at the Camber, Isle of Wight, Gosport and Southampton, where he made drawings of two liners the *Almazora* and *Alberta*. He took a week's holiday in Normandy, then in September returned to Southampton twice on painting expeditions, drew HMS *Nelson* at Portsmouth, did further work at Flathouse Quay and on the 12th drew the *Saxon*, a hay barge at the Camber. The next day he travelled to Wootton, Isle of Wight for the day with a fellow painter Dorian Smith. The diary records that on 6th September Anson's studio was blessed by Father Purcell. More time was now spent on painting, much of it indoors, writing invitations, preparing labels and framing for the exhibition which opened at Gardner, Albert & Co's Fine Art Gallery, 3 Pembroke Road. From October 5th to the 19th he stayed with the monks of Caldey Island. There are few entries between the 15th and 28th of the month, but enough overall to give a rounded picture of the man, the pattern of his religious observances, his love of company, his visits to exhibitions and the theatre, even his writing, for his earliest book, *The Pilgrim's Guide to Franciscan Italy* was published that same year, and the diary indicates he was already working on another, although his best remembered work *How To Draw Ships* did not appear until 1940, more than a decade later. A reviewer of Anson's 1927 exhibition made the point that, 'his abilities as a draughtsman come to the fore in studies of ships in Portsmouth,' so perhaps the foundations for much of his later success were laid in this decade of his life.

APPENDIX 4

William Fulljames was a student at Portsmouth College of Art between 1956 and 1961, the year he received his N.D.D. in sculpture and wood engraving.

'Memories are somewhat vague now, but I do remember that the painting department and Intermediate (Foundation Course now) students were in the main building behind the Guildhall. The sculpture department, graphics and dress design were in a place at Hilsea and the ceramics were done under a railway bridge next to the city morgue! This all changed of course when the new college opened in 1960.

Charlie Upton was in charge of the sculpture department. The teaching was pretty conservative and not terribly exciting. We did a lot of casting in cement-fondu with fibre glass, which was a relatively new material at the time. Wood engraving was taught by Gerry Tucker, and this department from that era has become quite well known among devotees of that medium. Hilary Paynter who was a friend and contemporary of mine is the chairman of the Society of Wood Engravers (South West England). Other pupils of Gerry Tucker who do, or have exhibited with the South West England yearly shows, are myself, Yvonne Elston, Shirley Mungapen, Garrick Palmer.

I remember that when I first went to the College we did a course called Basic Design which consisted mostly of building sort of model blocks of flats with coloured paper cubes! The Architectural College was affiliated to the Art College, and these tower blocks (full size) sprang up all over the place in the 60s!

What else comes to mind? We did regular life drawing which I appreciate and I still draw from the model. I am told that this sort of thing is discouraged now in art schools.

During my time Gaydon was the principal, Hayden head of painting. Jefferson, Smedley and Finley are names of teachers that come to mind. Smedley was rather a caustic character. He once told us we looked too smart to be art students and should dress more scruffily! He also used to make the girls cry when criticising their work! More important perhaps are my memories of Gerry Tucker and the wood engraving department.'

Bill Fulljames, Ibiza, July 2005.

APPENDIX 5

Select list of painters working in Portsmouth and the neighbourhood c.1770–c.1970.

Anson, Peter (1889–1975)

Atkins, William Edward (1842/3–1910)

Bray, Gabriel (1750–1823)

Calcott, James (fl.1837–c.1862)

Chambers, George (1803–1840)

Clevely, John junr. (1747–1786)

Coish, Harry (1857–1925)

Cole, George (1810–1883)

Cole, Vicat (1833–1893)

Cooke, Edward William (1811–1880)

Cunliffe, David (fl.1825–1856)

Daniell, William (1769–1837)

Dawson, Henry (1811–1878)

Downing, George (1878–1940)

Elliott, Robert (fl.1810–1849)

Elliott, William (fl.1790–1796)

Eurich, Richard (1903–1992)

Fergusson, John D. (1874–1961)

Garneray, Louis (1783–1850)

Gilbert, Joseph Francis (1792–1855)

Gilpin, William (1724–1804)

Goodwin, Sydney (1867–1944?)

Grant, William (1893–1982)

Green, John (living artist)

Horne, George (fl.1915–c.1940)

Jefferies, Wilfrid Avalon (1903–1970)

Jones, Thomas (1742–1803)

King, Edward (1862–1951)

Leslie, Robert (fl.1843–1887)

Livesay, John (fl.1799–1832)

Livesay, Richard (1750?–1826)

Luny, Thomas (1759–1857)

Mitchell, William Frederick (c.1839–1914?)

Northcote, James (1746–1831)

Palmer, Garrick (living artist)

Pearse, Violet (c.1900–c.1970)

Penley, Aaron Edwin (1807–1870)

Poate, Richard (fl.1845–c.1869)

Rimmington, Eric (living artist)

Rose, David T. (fl.1915–1938)

Rowlandson, Thomas (1756–1827)

Schetky, John Christian (1778–1874)

Serres, Dominic (1722–1786)

Shalders, George (1826–1873)

Smyth, William (1813–1888)

Snape, Martin (fl.1874–1901)

Stanfield, William Clarkson (1793–1867)

Steer, Philip Wilson (1860–1942)

Summers, Alick D. (1868–1938)

Tissot, James (1836–1902)

Turner, Joseph William Mallard (1775–1851)

Ubsdell, Richard Henry Clements (1813–1887)

Whistler, James Abbott McNeill (1834–1903)

Wyllie, William Lionel (1851–1931)

Young, E.H. (fl.1925–1930)

LIST OF ILLUSTRATIONS

Black and White

[within the text]

50. Harry Coish, *May Day Celebrations at Portsmouth, the procession passing through Fratton. Firemen leading followed by the Corporation horses*, n.d. Drawing, Portsmouth City Museums.

51. *Business Card for W.E. Atkins*, n.d. Printed, Portsmouth City Records Office.

52. W.E. Atkins, *The Reserve Squadron Reviewed by Queen Victoria*, 1878. Watercolour, Portsmouth City Museums.

53. *Tower House*, 1919. Private Collection.

54. *W.L. Wyllie Working in his Studio, Tower House*, c.1928. Private Collection.

55. J.D. Fergusson, *Portsmouth Docks*, 1918. Oil, University of Stirling, Fergusson Collection, courtesy of The Fergusson Gallery, Perth & Kinross Council.

56. Martin Snape, *Globe Yard, Oyster Street*, n.d. Postcard, Portsmouth City Museums.

57. Alick Summers, *The Guildhall from Commercial Road*, 1936. Watercolour, Portsmouth City Museums.

58. Peter Anson, *The Camber, Portsmouth*, 1929. Pen and ink, The Moray Council Museums Service O L1979 18gc.

59. Martin Snape, *The Camber Dock and Electricity Generating Station*, 1894. Watercolour, Portsmouth City Museums.

60. George Horne, *Palmerston Road*, c.1932. Etching, Portsmouth City Museums.

61. Edward King, *Hampshire and Jubilee Terraces*, 1941/3. Oil on board, Portsmouth City Museums.

62. Edward King, *Ruins of St Thomas's Street*, 1941/3. Oil on board, Portsmouth City Museums.

63. Edward King, *Guildhall, from Russell Street, Southsea* 1941/3. Oil on board, Portsmouth City Museums.

64. Edward King, *Houseboat at Milton alongside a Quay with a Girl in Red*, 1946. Oil on board, Portsmouth City Museums.

65. Violet Pearse, *Commercial Road, Portsmouth*, 1943. Pen and ink, Portsmouth City Museums.

66. W.A. Jefferies, *The Construction of a Floating Dock, HM Dockyard, Portsmouth*, 1966. Watercolour, Portsmouth City Museums.

67. W.A. Jefferies, *Navigation Light*, c.1963. Watercolour, Portsmouth City Museums.

68. John Green, *Yard Boy Rigger*, 2003. Pen and wash. © John Green.

69. *Portsmouth College of Art*, 1960. University of Portsmouth.

70. *The Library, Portsmouth College of Art*, 1960. University of Portsmouth.

Colour
[plates in colour section]

1. George Chambers, *Entrance to Portsmouth Harbour*, 1835. Watercolour, Portsmouth City Museums.

2. William Daniell, *View from Portsdown Hill*, 1823. Aquatint, Portsmouth City Museums.

3. William Grant, *Langstone Mill*, n.d. Watercolour, Private Collection.

4. John Clevely Junr., *View of His Majesty's Dockyard at Portsmouth*, n.d. Coloured engraving, Portsmouth City Museums.

5. Anon, *Town Hall from the North East*, 1830. Watercolour, Portsmouth City Museums.

6. John Swete, *Gosport Hospital*, 'from the Great Cabbin of the *Royal George*', 1777. Pen and wash(?) Courtesy of the Royal Institution of Cornwall, Courtney Library, DJS/2/1.

7. Louis Garneray, *Prison Hulks in Portsmouth Harbour*, c.1810. Oil, Portsmouth City Museums.

8. R.H.C. Ubsdell, *July 22 1847 Abolition of Free Mart Fair*. Watercolour, Portsmouth City Museums.

9. Thomas Rowlandson, *Portsmouth Point*, c.1800. Watercolour, Portsmouth City Museums.

10. Richard Livesay, *Military Review of the Worcestershire Regiment by Major-General Whitelock, 14 October 1800, on Southsea Common*. Oil on canvas, Portsmouth City Museums.

11. J.C. Schetky, *Portsmouth Harbour*, 1822. Sepia wash drawing, Portsmouth City Museums.

12. J.M.W. Turner, *The Disembarkation of Louis–Philippe at Portsmouth*, c.1844-5. Watercolour, © Tate, London 2008.

13. W. Clarkson Stanfield, *Entrance to Portsmouth Harbour*, 1829. Watercolour, Portsmouth City Museums.

14. George Cole, *The London Road, Portsdown Hill*, 1867. Oil on canvas, Portsmouth City Museums.

15. R.H.C. Ubsdell, *Volunteer Review*, 1868. Watercolour, Portsmouth City Museums.

16. Richard Poate, *Dr W.C. Engledue, chairman at the banquet held in 9.1856 to welcome home other ranks from the Crimea, proposing the Royal Toast*. Oil on canvas, Portsmouth City Museums.

17. William Smyth, *On the Point, Portsmouth*, 1857. Oil on canvas, Portsmouth City Museums.

18. James Tissot, *Portsmouth Dockyard*, c.1877. Oil, © Tate, London 2008.

19. W.E. Atkins, *Panoramic View from the Black Horse Tavern to Victoria Pier*, 1884. Watercolour, Portsmouth City Museums.

20. W.E. Atkins, *Hay Barge*, n.d. Watercolour, Portsmouth City Museums.

21. W.L. Wyllie, *Old Hulks, Portsmouth*, 1880. Oil on canvas, Portsmouth City Museums.

22. J.D. Fergusson, *Blue Submarine, Portsmouth*, 1918. Oil on canvas, courtesy of The Fergusson Gallery, Perth & Kinross Council.

23. W.L. Wyllie, *Spit Fort*, 1931. Watercolour, Portsmouth City Museums.

24. W.L. Wyllie, *H.M.S. 'Victory' and H.M.S. 'Renown'*, 1928. Print, Portsmouth City Museums.

25. W. Marston Derrick, *Clarence Pier*, 1897. Watercolour, Portsmouth City Museums.

26. Alick Summers, *Point, Portsmouth*, 1936. Watercolour, Portsmouth City Museums.

27. Eric Ravilious, *The Ward Room (2)*, 1940. Graphite with watercolour, Collections Imperial War Museum © DACS.

28. Edward King, *The Connaught Drill Hall, Stanhope Road*, 1941/2. Oil on board, Portsmouth City Museums.

29. Edward King, *The Grounds of St James's Hospital*, n.d. Oil on board, Portsmouth City Museums.

30. Eric Rimmington, *Trafalgar House Mural*, 1949 (Detail). Oils on a white oil undercoat. Photograph by Alex Saunderson.

31. W.A. Jefferies, *Car Ferry to the Isle of Wight*, c.1959. Pen, ink and watercolour, Portsmouth City Museums.

32. John Green, *Cruiser in No.16 Dock*, 2002. Watercolour. © John Green.

SELECT BIBLIOGRAPHY

Books are published in London, unless otherwise stated.

Anson, P.F., *Harbour Head, Maritime Memories*, 1945.

Archibald, E.H.H., *Dictionary of Sea Painters*, Woodbridge, 1980.

Artist Adventurers in Eighteenth Century India: Thomas and William Daniell, Ex. Catalogue, Spink & Son Ltd., London, 12–29 Nov., 1974.

Auerbach E., and Adams, C. Kingsley, *Paintings and Sculpture at Hatfield House*, 1971.

Ayton R., and Daniell, W., *A Voyage Round Great Britain With A Series of Views Illustrative of the Character and Prominent Features of the Coast*, 8v., 1814–1828, VI1.

Baker, C. Jane, *Thomas Luny (1759–1837)*, Ex. Catalogue, Royal Albert Memorial Museum, Exeter 22 July–25 September, 1982.

Barringer, T.J., *The Cole Family, Painters of the English Landscape 1835–1975*, Ex. Catalogue Portsmouth City Museum, 1987.

Batey, M., 'The New Forest and the Picturesque,' in Gill Hedley and Adrian Rance (eds.,), *The Gardens and Landscapes of Hampshire*, Horndean Hampshire, 1987, pp.40–47.

Buckman, D., *The Dictionary Of Artists In Britain Since 1945*, Bristol, 1998.

Burton L., and Musselwhite B., *The Portsmouth Harbour Story*, Tiverton, 2000.

Carus, Dr. G.C. (Trans. S.C. Davison), *The King of Saxony's Journey Through England And Scotland In The Year 1844*, 1846.

A Catalogue Of The Beautiful Collection of FIRST CLASS PAINTINGS, Choice sketches and studies of MR GEORGE COLE, (who is removing to London) Which Will be sold By Auction By CROOK AND SON, At The Studio, Pembroke Street, on Wednesday, October the 20th 1852, Portsea 1852.

Cave, K., Garlick, K., and Macintyre, A.,(eds.,), *The Diary of Joseph Farington*, 16v., New Haven U.S.A., and London, 1978–1984, XIV, XV.

Charpentier, W.H., *THE NEW PORTSMOUTH, SOUTHSEA, Anglesey & Hayling Island Guide*, Portsmouth, 1837.

Charpentier's *Guide to Portsmouth And Southsea, Illustrated With a Map*, Portsmouth, 1912.

Chigwell, R., *The Life And Paintings of Vicat Cole, R.A.*, 4v., 1898.

City Museum & Bashford Portrait Gallery: A Brief Guide For the Use Of Visitors, Portsmouth, 1935/6.

Clarke, M., *The Tempting Prospect A Social History Of English Watercolours*, 1981.

Concise Catalogue of Oil Paintings in the National Maritime Museum, compiled by the Staff, Woodbridge, 1985.

Cordingley, D., *Nicholas Pocock 1740–1821*, 1986.

Cumyns, the Rev. B.H., *The Ancient and Modern History of Portsmouth, Portsea, Gosport and their Environs*, 1799.

Denvir, B., *The Eighteenth Century Art, Design and Society, 1689–1789*, 1983.

    - *The Early Nineteenth Century Art, Design and Society, 1789–1852*, 1984.

    - *The Late Victorians Art, Design and Society, 1852–1910*, 1986.

Descriptive CATALOGUE Of The Paintings By ancient And Modern Masters, Water-Colour Drawings &c. &c. In THE MUSEUM Of The Portsmouth & Portsea Literary & Philosophical Society, With Which The Proprietors Have Favored The Institution, Portsmouth, 1826.

De Walden, Lord Howard, and Lavers Smith H., B.A., (eds.,), *The Reminiscences of Henry Angelo*, 2v., 1904.

Egerton, J., *Making & Meaning: Turner The Fighting Téméraire*, Ex. Catalogue, National Gallery, London, 1995.

Fawcett, T., *The Rise of English Provincial Art Artists, Patrons and Institutions outside London 1800–1830*, Oxford, 1974.

Foss, B., *War Paint: Art, War, State and Identity in Britain 1939–1945*, New Haven U.S.A. and London, 2007.

Fremantle, A., *The Wynne Diaries* 3v., 1936–40, II.

Friedman, J., 'Every Lady Her Own Drawing Master', *Apollo*, CV, April 1977, pp.262–267.

Garlick, K., *Joseph Farington*, Ex. Catalogue, Bolton Museum and Art Gallery, 1977.

Garneray, L., (trans. Wood, L.), *The French Prisoner*, 1957.

Gates, W.G., *Illustrated History of Portsmouth*, Portsmouth, 1900.

Gillett, P., *The Victorian Painter's World*, Gloucester, 1990.

Goodwin, P., *The Ships of Trafalgar: The British, French and Spanish Fleets October 1805*, 2005.

Greenaway, W., 'Artistic Passion For Sea And Ships John Christian Schetky And His work', *Country Life*, CXXII, 10 April 1980, pp.1133–1134.

Grundy, N.J.H., *W.L. Wyllie, R.A., The Portsmouth Years*, Portsmouth Paper No.68, Portsmouth, 1996.

Haggerty, J.H.M., 'Edward R. King: The Portsmouth Painter Who Influenced Van Gogh,' B.A. Hons. Dissertation, School of Art, Design and Visual Culture, University of Portsmouth, 2001.

Hamnett, Nina, *Laughing Torso*, 1984.

Hampshire County Council, *William Grant, Exhibition Of Havant Watercolours*, Ex. Catalogue, Havant Museum 30th November–7th December 1994.

Hardie, M., *Water-Colour Painting In Britain*, 3v., 1968, III, Appendix .

Harris, R.G., 'R.Poate of Portsmouth Artist and Photographer,' *Journal of the Society for Army Historical Research*, LXVIII, No.273, Spring 1990, pp.1–6.

Heywood, A., *Guide To Portsmouth, Southsea, Portsea & Landport with A Tide Table*, 1876?

Hickman, P., 'Fresh Light on Lea of Portsmouth,' *Country Life*, 16 Jan. 1969, pp.122–123.

Hooker, D., *Nina Hamnett Queen of Bohemia*, 1987.

Hollingsworth, H., *The Portsmouth Guide*, Portsmouth, 1823.

Hoad, M.J., *Portsmouth As Others Have Seen It, Part I, 1540–1790*, Portsmouth Paper No.15, Portsmouth, 1972.
        - *Part II, 1790–1900*, Portsmouth Paper No.20, Portsmouth, 1973.

Hope Moncrieff, A. (ed.), *A Guide To The Watering-Places And Health Resorts Of England, Scotland, Ireland, And Wales* (1892).

Howard, P., 'Painters' preferred places', *Journal of Historical Geography*, II, 2, 1965, pp.138–154.

Howgego, J.L., *Edward William Cooke R.A., F.R.S., F.Z.S., F.S.A.*, Ex. Catalogue, Guildhall Art Gallery, London, 1970.

Hyde R., *Panoramania! The Art And Entertainment Of The 'All-Embracing' View*, Barbican Art Gallery, London, 1988/89.

James, H., *English Hours*, 1960.

Johnson, Brigadier R.F, *The Royal George*, 1971.

Leslie, R.C., *A Sea Painter's Log*, 1885.

  – *A Water-Biography*, 1894.

Lewis, H., *Lewis's Illustrated Hand-Book of Portsmouth and Guide To The Royal Dockyard, Harbour, Haslar Hospital, Gosport, Fortifications & Portsmouth*, 1860.

Lincoln, M , 'Naval Ship Launches As Public Spectacles 1773–1854,' *The Mariner's Mirror*, 83 No.4, Nov. 1997, pp.466–472.

Locknam, A., *The Etchings Of James McNeill Whistler*, 1984.

Long, P., with Cumming, E., *The Scottish Colourists 1900–1930*, National Galleries of Scotland, Edinburgh in association with the Royal Academy of Arts, London, 2000.

MacColl, D.S., *Life, Work And Setting of Philip Wilson Steer*, 1945.

Magrath, P.A., *Fort Cumberland 1747–1850: Key to an Island's Defence,* Portsmouth Paper No.60, Portsmouth 1992.

Mallalieu, H.L., *The Dictionary of British Water Colour Artists up to 1920*, 2v., Woodbridge, 1980.

Marshall, N.R., and Warner, W., *James Tissot Victorian Life/Modern Love*, New Haven U.S.A. & London, 1999.

Martin, R., 'Martin Snape – Gosport's Celebrated Artist' *Hampshire Gardens Trust Journal*, No.17, Autumn 1998, pp.27–29.

McInnes, R., *The Garden Isle Landscape Paintings Of The Isle of Wight 1790–1920*, Ventnor, 1990.

  – *A Picturesque Tour Of The Isle of Wight*, Ventnor, 1993.

Measum, G., *The Official Illustrated Guide To the Brighton And South Coast Railways And their Branches*, n.d.

Merwe, P. van der, *Clarkson Stanfield*, Ex. Catalogue Tyne and Wear County Council Museum, Bonn Rheinishes Landesmuseum, and Sunderland Museum and Art Gallery, 1979.

Morris, M., *The Art Of J.D. Fergusson*, 1974.

Munday, J., *E.W. Cooke 1811–1880 A Man of his Time*, Woodbridge, 1996.

N.U.T. Conference Souvenir 1937 Portsmouth, 1937.

The Original Portsmouth Picture Show, Ex. Catalogue, Portsmouth City Museum, 1986.

Ousby, I., *The Englishman's England, Taste travel and the rise of tourism*, Cambridge, 1990.

Patterson, B.H., *"Give'er a cheer Boys" The Great Docks of Portsmouth Dockyard 1830–1914*, Portsmouth Royal Dockyard Historical Society, Publication No.5, 1989.

The Portsmouth Scene, 1, 2, 3, Ex. Catalogues, Portsmouth City Museum, 1960, 1961, 1980.

Powers, A., *Eric Ravilious, Imagined Realities*, Ex. Catalogue, Imperial War Museum, London, 2003.

Quail, S., and Stedman, J., *Images of Portsmouth*, Derby, 1973.

Quail, S., *Southsea Past*, Chichester, 2000.

Quarm, R., 'An Album Of Drawings By Gabriel Bray RN, HMS Pallas, 1774-5', *The Mariner's Mirror*, 81 No.1, Feb.1995, pp.32–44.

Quarm R., and Wyllie, J., *W.L. Wyllie, Marine Artist 1851–1931*, 1981.

Riely, J., *Rowlandson Drawings from The Paul Mellon Collection*, Ex. Catalogue, the Paul Mellon Collection, Yale Center For British Art, Newhaven U.S.A., and the Royal Academy of Arts, London, 1977.

Riley, R.C., *The Growth Of Southsea as a Naval Satellite And Victorian Resort*, Portsmouth Paper No.16, Portsmouth, 1972.

  – *Portsmouth, Ships Dockyard And Town*, Stroud, 2002.

Rothenstein, Sir J., *An Introduction to English Painting*, 2001.

Rimmington, E. 'The mural in Trafalgar House, Edinburgh Road, Portsmouth', *The Portsmouth Society – News*, 22nd May 2002, n.p.

Roe, S., (ed.,), *Oil Paintings in Public Ownership: Imperial War Museum*, 2006.

Roe, S., (ed.,), *Oil Paintings in Public Ownership: Southampton & the Isle of Wight*, 2007.

Roe, S., (ed.,), *Oil Paintings in Public Ownership in Hampshire*, 2007.

Rogers, H.T., *Martin Snape*, Gosport Historic Records and Museum Society, No.4 May 1972, pp.18–20.

Saunders, W.H., *The Annals Of Portsmouth*, 1880.

Schetky, S.F.L., *Ninety Years of Work and Play Sketches From the Public and Private Career of John Christian Schetky*, 1877.

Scott Hughes, J., *Harbours Of the Solent*, 1956.

Shanes, E., *Turner's England 1810–1838*, 1990.

Shawe-Taylor, D., *The Georgians Eighteenth Century Portraiture & Society*, 1990.

Sloan, K., *'A Noble Art' Amateur Artists and Drawing Masters c.1600–1800*, Ex.Catalogue, British Museum, London, 2000.

Smiles, S. and Pidgley, M., *The Perfection Of England Artist Visitors to Devon c.1750–1870*, Ex. Catalogue Royal Albert Memorial Museum, Exeter and Djanogly Art Gallery, University of Nottingham, 1995.

Stanfield, C., *Stanfield's Coast Scenery. A series Of Picturesque Views in the British Channel And On the Coast Of France, From Original Drawings Taken Expressly for The Work*, 1836.

Stedman, J., *Portsmouth Reborn Destruction & Reconstruction 1939–1974*, Portsmouth Paper No.66, Portsmouth 1995.

Steegman, J., 'Aaron Penley – A Forgotton Water-Colourist,' *Apollo*, LXVII No.395 Jan.1958, pp.14–17.

Stewart B., and Cutten, M., *Chichester Artists 1530–1900*, Canterbury, 1987.

Strong, Sir R., *And When Did You Last See Your Father?*, 1978.

Sumner A., and Smith G., *Thomas Jones (1742–1803) An Artist Rediscovered*. Ex. Catalogue, Yale in Association with National Museums and Galleries of Wales, Cardiff, Manchester, London, 2003.

Surry, N., *Art In A Dockyard Town: Portsmouth 1770–1845*, Portsmouth Paper No.59, Portsmouth 1992.

- 'James Northcote at Portsmouth,' *'The Burlington Magazine*, 136 No.1093, April 1994, pp.234–237.
- 'Artistic Developments In Portsmouth and Plymouth 1740–1830,' *The Hatcher Review*, Four, No. 40, Autumn 1995, pp.33–45.

Taswell, L., *The Portsmouth Guide*, 1775.

Taylor, J., *Marine Painting Images of Sail, Sea and Shore*, 1995.

Thomas, J.H., 'Portsmouth Naval Academy: An Educational Experiment Examined', *Portsmouth Archives Review*, 3, 1978, pp.10–39.

Tickner, L., *Modern Life & Modern Subjects: British Art in the Early Twentieth Century*, 2000.

Tisdall, J., *Joshua Cristall: in search of Arcadia*, Hereford, 1995.

Treuheuz, J., *Hard Times, Social Realism in Victorian Art*, Ex. Catalogue Manchester City Art Gallery, 1987.

Turley, R.V., *A Directory of Hampshire & Isle of Wight Art*, Southampton, 1977.

Ullman, A., (ed.,), *Ravilious at War*, Huddersfield, 2002.

Wade, G.R., *The Winds of Change: Naval Reviews At Spithead 1842–56*, Portsmouth Paper, No.49, Portsmouth, 1987.

Ward Lock & Co., *A Pictorial and Descriptive Guide To Southsea And Portsmouth*, 1929/30.

Wark, R.R., *Rowlandson's Drawings For A Tour In A Post Chaise*, San Marino, California, 1963.

Warrell, I., *Turner and Venice*, Tate Britain Ex. Catalogue, 2003.

Waterhouse, Sir E., *The Dictionary of British 18th Century Painters*, Woodbridge, 1981.

Webb, J., *An Early Victorian Street: The High Street, Old Portsmouth*, Portsmouth Paper No.26, Portsmouth 1977.

  - *Portsmouth Free Mart Fair The Last Phase 1800–1847*, Portsmouth Paper No.35, Portsmouth 1982.

  - *Sir Frederic Madden and Portsmouth*, Portsmouth Paper No.47, Portsmouth 1987.

Webb J., Quail, S., Haskell, P., & Riley, R., *The Spirit of Portsmouth: A History*, Chichester, 1989.

Wilcox, S., 'The Wider Sea: Marine Watercolours and Landscape Art', in *Masters of the Sea*, Ex. Catalogue National Maritime Museum and Yale Center for British Art, 1987, pp.37–68.

Williams, H., *Henry Dawson (1811–1878)*, Centenary Ex. Catalogue, Nottingham University Art Gallery, 1978.

Wood, C., *The Dictionary of Victorian Painters*, 2v., Woodbridge, 1995.

Wyllie, M.A., *We Were One. A Life Of W.L. Wyllie R.A., R.E., R.I.,* 1935.

Yates, N., *Selling Southsea, Promoting Portsmouth, 1920–2000*, Portsmouth Paper No.72, Portsmouth, 2002.

Yates, R.W. (ed.), 'From Wooden Walls To Dreadnoughts In A Lifetime', *The Mariner's Mirror* 48, No.4 Nov. 1962, pp.291–303.

INDEX OF ARTISTS

Page references in bold type refer to illustrations, those in colour are prefixed by **pl.**